SHARING THE BREAD OF LIFE

Chuck —
Good friend +
Loving Supporter.
Love + Hope,

Ed Loring

910 PONCE DE LEON AVENUE. ABOVE, 2005; RIGHT, 1982

SHARING THE BREAD OF LIFE

Hospitality and Resistance at the Open Door Community

Peter R. Gathje

Calvin Kimbrough
PHOTOGRAPHY EDITOR

The Open Door Community
Atlanta
2006

The Open Door Community, Atlanta 30306
 Published 2006
Printed in the United States of America

13 12 11 10 09 08 07 06 5 4 3 2 1

ISBN-10: 0-9715893-2-1
ISBN-13: 978-0-9715893-2-2

With gratitude to Ed Loring and Murphy Davis, friends, mentors and witnesses in Christian discipleship; to past and present members of the Open Door Community who have embodied Jesus' liberating call to be with the poor and to struggle for justice; and especially to my teachers from the streets and prisons from whom I continue to learn of God's graciousness and human compassion

CONTENTS

WILLIE DEE WIMBERLY

PROLOGUE

FOR NEARLY TWENTY YEARS I have been coming to the Open Door Community. The Open Door was initially a place for me to do research. Back in 1987, I was a student at Emory University's Candler School of Theology. In search of a master's thesis topic, I had proposed to my advisor that I write an analysis of the Christian ethics of Jerry Falwell. This seemed worthwhile to me, given the influence of the Religious Right at the time. My advisor, Dr. Hendrikus Boers, did not agree. He said, "Why don't you write about 'real Christians.'" When I asked him if he knew any, he suggested the Open Door. The rest, as they say, "is history." I started volunteering at the Open Door in the Winter of 1987, and then came to live in the community for six weeks in the early summer. I got

ABOVE PHOTOGRAPH © KARIN HEREZER

plenty of material for my theological analysis of the community and its history, and have been coming back ever since. My thesis became the book, *Christ Comes in the Stranger's Guise.*

The transformation of my master's thesis into a history of the Open Door Community was the idea of Ed Loring and Murphy Davis, two of the founders of the Open Door. The transformation of my life that began at the Open Door was the work of the whole community, and the people they serve, and I believe the gracious and liberating God who works through us all.

The Open Door Community has been a place of transformation for many people in its twenty-five years of existence. For those who founded the community, those who have become partners, the many resident volunteers, the residents from the streets and prisons, the people who come from the streets for meals, showers, clothes, for everyone who comes to the Open Door it is a place where change takes place. The Open Door is a living, dynamic, welcoming, enlivening, sometimes infuriating, and always surprising place.

My first experience with the Open Door as a place of transformation came when I went with community members to help serve breakfast to homeless persons in the basement of the Butler Street C.M.E. Church. At that time, this was where the Open Door served its weekday breakfasts. I had met with Ed about a week before to make my proposal for doing research about the community. And Ed had made clear that if I was going to do this research then I needed to enter as fully as possible into the life and work of the community. His emphasis fit exactly with my desire to do "participant observation," and I also let him know that I had a little experience with living in community since I had been a Benedictine monk at one point.

But now was the moment of truth, actually going to help serve at the breakfast. I was filled with trepidation. I had no previous contact with homeless people except seeing them occasionally on the streets, and I didn't know any of the community members. On the way to the church, the Open Door's old green van stalled at almost every intersection. The driver, Dietrich Gerstner, came to the community from Germany. His driving might have been acceptable on the "autobahn" but it was terrifying on the streets of Atlanta. Along the way I was regaled with stories of disasters that had occurred on other mornings while serving breakfast. It was, I found out later, typical of the humor in the community where stories are often told in such a way that community members support each other in the sorrow and fears faced in the work. That morning it simply made me more anxious.

But the whole experience also started to work on my heart and my mind. In speaking with other volunteers over the next several months, I found my fears that morning were not so unusual. The homeless initially seem so different from those who, like me, come from more economically secure backgrounds to volunteer at shelters or soup kitchens. By serving at this breakfast I began to know people, instead of "the homeless." I began to hear their stories, and I began to realize not only the complexities of the persons and their situations, but also that each of them is a human being who is surviving as best they know how under extremely inhumane circumstances. At Butler Street I met men, women, and on some mornings, children, who were incredibly friendly and forgiving in the face of horrendous conditions. Over the next few years as I continued to volunteer at the Open Door, I also occasionally encountered some very angry persons, mad at being cold and hungry and rejected. Though it was hard to be on the receiving end of their anger, I knew I'd be angry, too, being on the streets. I also met people struggling with addictions and/or mental illness; struggles made worse by the neglect they suffered as homeless persons.

I was experiencing a world I had not taken the time to learn about before. The distance between me and the poor was slowly being reduced. I had been occasionally involved with "peace and justice" issues before, but now the people I was serving and talking with were not an "issue"—they were people. My education in something I later learned to identify as Catholic Worker "personalism" was beginning. The community members and other volunteers in the way they served, and the people I was serving, were teaching me about respect for each person as a child of God, about respect for the human dignity of each as embodying Christ's presence.

This respect for human dignity also began to raise questions about justice. How could there be lines of people every morning for breakfast in a country as rich as the United States? Why would Atlanta, the "city too busy to hate," find it so easy to spend millions of federal, state, and local tax dollars for business, athletic, and upscale residential development, but be unwilling to house and care for homeless persons, or even to provide public bathrooms? Why did so many people favor public policies that reflected fear and hatred of the poor?

My experience with the transforming power of the prison ministry of the Open Door did not come until I moved into the Open Door. This ministry had at first seemed distant from the work at Butler Street. But then it became terribly concrete. Four executions were conducted by the state of Georgia in the six weeks I initially lived at the Open Door. The men killed were close to the community, especially to Murphy Davis, who is central to the community's prison ministry. The Open Door led vigils of protest at the state capitol building before each execution. I got my first taste of the hatred and viciousness of death penalty supporters who cursed and made obscene gestures. One of the men executed requested that the Open Door conduct his funeral. I helped to carry his casket to the grave at Jubilee Partners, an intentional Christian community in close relationship with the Open Door. The death penalty also went from being an "issue" to being about persons with human dignity as children of God.

The Open Door was teaching me how to practice the works of mercy: feeding the hungry, giving drink to the thirsty, visiting the sick, liberating the captive, and burying the dead. I learned to start reading the Bible in a way that takes Jesus seriously at his word. Why hadn't it sunk into my thick head before that following Jesus meant doing those things, meant being compassionate to the vulnerable, and meant recognizing Jesus in the poor?

I was also learning that the Bible teaches that mercy without justice is a hollow manner in which to serve the poor who come as Christ. In the Open Door's reading of the Bible, informed by its life with the poor, love expressed in works of mercy is the basis of justice and its fulfillment. Both works of mercy and works of justice are essential in the Christian life. In serving meals to homeless persons or visiting prisoners, the Open Door anticipates a time of justice when there will be plenty for all and no one will be cast out from community. These works of mercy are seen as sacraments, embodying the justice that is sought. Thus, the Open Door always connects its works of mercy with calls for a more just society, for the creation of the beloved community of which Martin Luther King, Jr. spoke.

Another way I began to be transformed by the Open Door was to become bolder about calling for justice. During the first time that I lived at the Open Door I went with community members once a week to Woodruff Park in downtown Atlanta. There we handed out leaflets concerning the destruction of Plaza Park and its effect on the homeless. The park had long been a place of refuge for homeless persons and it was being destroyed for the construction of Underground Atlanta. The community was urging the city to develop a green space to replace Plaza Park, a place where the homeless could find some respite and would not be harassed by the police. The community was also pressing the city to meet the needs of the homeless for public restrooms and other facilities instead of confronting homeless persons with punitive measures such as a "vagrant free zone" in the downtown area.

Banging on soup pots, singing spirituals and protest songs, I marched with the community from the park to city hall. More leaflets were handed out and a mini-rally was held on the steps. The actions always generated a lot of attention. It seemed to provide a constant reminder to downtown shoppers and business people that business as usual in the city was leaving people on the streets. Often it was a reminder that irritated the lunchtime crowd in the park. I often felt foolish. Wanting to be "normal" dies hard.

But that was another part of my transformation. I was learning that "normal" as defined by the dominant society is a lie and is death-dealing. And I was learning that being odd is life-giving and that Flannery O'Connor was right, "You shall know the truth and it shall make you odd." I now believe that what has kept me coming back over all these years is just how life giving (and odd) it is to be at the Open Door. There is a depth to life at the Open Door that is invigorating and life-changing. The power of the evil confronted in the realities of homelessness and prison and the death penalty is countered by something more powerful—the graciousness of God. To be at the Open Door is to enter into that biblical drama, and thus to be joined to the promise of Jesus who came to give us life to the full (John 10:10).

And, part of that depth of life is the enriching diversity of the community itself which challenges the evils of racism, classism, and sexism. The resident volunteers and members of the community from the streets and prisons are old, middle-aged, and young; white and black; male and female; gay and straight; those with college degrees and those struggling to pass the G.E.D. Community life is never dull. The variety of experiences sometimes causes tension, but it also provides the background for incredibly rich conversations. Not to mention silliness. People living at the Open Door know how to smile and to joke. Those without a sense of humor don't last long. The colors and fashion of the community are evident on "Mardi Gras" when everyone dons the gaudiest, wildest, and most outrageous costumes gleaned from the donation box. Birthdays provide not only a rare treat of cake and ice cream, but also opportunity for stories that "roast" the birthday person and the demand that he or she "say something intelligent." Halloween brings visits to the clothes closet where community members weave a nightmare out of donated finery. And one never quite gets over the ironic and joyful conviction in Ed Loring's occasional shouts, such as "It won't be long now!" or "Justice is important, but supper is essential!" In fact, if you want the embodiment of "odd" as coming from truth-telling and "odd" as life giving, spend some time with Ed.

When I joined community members for twenty-four hours on the streets another essential part of my transformation took place. Although the Open Door recognizes that these twenty-four hours on the streets are symbolic, during this time I experienced a small taste of the hardships homeless people regularly face. It helped to reduce the distance between those of us who are not homeless and those who are. Exhaustion, hunger, and cold marked my time on the streets. I saw an Atlanta that was not advertised by downtown business interests represented by Central Atlanta Progress, Olympic organizers, and corporate powers like Coca-Cola. For the "normal" world, Atlanta is a success story. From the perspective of those on the streets, it is an abysmal failure. I was told to "move along," slept in an overcrowded and dirty shelter, stood in line for food, and desperately sought to find a place where I could get warm.

Another part of my transformation has come at the Open Door's times for prayer and worship. Raised a Catholic in the Midwest, I was not exactly a hand clapping, shoutin' out, kind of worshiper. I could hardly pray without a prayerbook. I can clap my hands more or less in time with a song now (with concentrated effort), and whisper a shout or two, and can also be coaxed to "share a prayer concern." What I have learned is that prayer is both serious business and joyous. Talking with and praising God is not to be taken lightly, but it is also a time of great joy and thanksgiving. The Open Door in its weekly Eucharist, daily gatherings for prayer at meals, before and after serving homeless persons, before going to a protest, knows how to pray and worship. The prayer of the community is the heart of the community's life; all flows from and returns back into prayer. The gracious meaning of the life together is affirmed and celebrated as community members draw connections between the Eucharist and the soup kitchen, between Baptism and showers, between the ritualized washing of feet and the Thursday night foot clinic. There is in the Open Door Community a wholistic connecting of prayer and work, just as there is an integrity between works of mercy and works of justice. The community constantly affirms that faith and daily life are a continuum.

I have come to see in the Open Door Community the life of Christian discipleship that begins with a response to Jesus' call to be with those marginalized by the powerful, to know and serve God by knowing and serving the poor. I have found at the Open Door people who have been called by God to leave behind their human securities and entrust their lives to this God who is found among the poor. I am thankful that I have been invited into their journey.

The story of the Open Door Community begins with the deepening Christian discipleship of four persons: Murphy Davis, Ed Loring, Carolyn and Rob Johnson. Each was raised in mainline Christian churches that rested more or less easily with American life in general and Southern life in particular. But their experiences during the 1960s with the Civil Rights, Peace, and Feminist Movements, along with contact with a tradition of radical Christianity, made them critical of both mainline church life and American society. This critique deepened as they came to see the destructive tendencies of this society in the inhumane conditions imposed upon the homeless and the imprisoned. They sought a Gospel alternative to a society structured by self-interest, individualism and consumerism. Drawing upon various aspects of the tradition of radical Christian faith, they realized that a community shaped by the Gospel and its call to peace and justice could provide a powerful context for resistance and transformation. The Open Door Community was thus born.

The Open Door stands within and draws upon the tradition of Christian communities founded upon Christ's proclamation of the alternative vision of the Reign of God—what Martin Luther King, Jr., called "the Beloved Community." Such communities, by the character of their lives together, witness to this vision and challenge the ethos of the broader church and society. The early church stood in resistance to the Roman Empire, refusing to conform to a society organized around imperial idolatry and domination. The early monastic movements resisted the domestication of the Christian faith in the Constantinian era of increasing cooperation between church and empire. Later, Benedictine monasticism preserved the peace and hospitality of Christ amidst the bloody chaos of the disintegration of Roman society. St. Francis and his followers called the church of Christendom to remember Gospel solidarity with the poor rather than to continue playing into the politics of the rich and powerful. Radical reformers such as Menno Simons summoned Christians in the 16th century away from Christendom and toward peacemaking and simple living along the lines of the early church recorded in the

Acts of Apostles. In a similar manner, the Quakers advocated an unadorned faith, and rejected slavery as incompatible with the Christian faith. And too, there was the Black Church that emerged in opposition to slavery and racism and in affirmation of the dignity of African Americans, and provided the soil for the Civil Rights Movement and other struggles for liberation.

The spirit of all these communities of faith has been carried forward in such communities as the Catholic Worker Movement, Koinonia Farm, Sojourners Community, and the Community for Creative Nonviolence. At the Open Door many elements of that tradition and these communities are evident: charismatic leadership; the belief that a small community can provide support for and witness to the need for profound social change; and tensions between the vision and the ongoing power of the existing cultural and institutional order. Aware of this tradition, and these communities, and drawing upon their resources, the Open Door Community recognizes the power of the Gospel shared in common life to form people of peace, truth and justice. In community, people can live and work together to encourage one another in a Gospel-based way of life and to oppose the values and social structures that deal death and attempt absolute rule over human life.

Something very appealing about the Open Door is that members of the community openly confess that they struggle to live this life of intense Christian discipleship. Such discipleship requires a recognition and rejection of the powerful idols set up in American society to take the place of the God of Jesus: idols of national security, of conspicuous consumption, of putting profits before people, of race and class. Conversion means no longer relying on those idols for their sense of identity and security. It means relying on the God who stands with the poor in love and demands justice. As the Open Door Community hears the Word of God, Christian discipleship means turning away from what is generally conceived of as success—as normal—

and turning toward life with the hungry, the homeless, and the imprisoned. The community remains a precarious experiment in love, for it stands against the "powers and principalities" in American society that seek the destruction of human dignity and thus deny God's intent for human life.

The Open Door Community seeks to live this Christian discipleship in the tradition of radical Christian faith in the urban setting of Atlanta, Georgia. In the past forty years Atlanta has rapidly grown to become one of the largest urban centers in the South, and indeed, the nation. It presents stunning contrasts of wealth and poverty, booming development and wealth set against a large segment of the population falling below the poverty level. It prides itself as the birthplace of Martin Luther King, Jr., and as a place where African-Americans hold political power, yet white dominated corporations and businesses still wield a dominant amount of the city's economic power. Whether white or black, this political and economic elite gives lip service to Dr. King while ignoring his commitment to economic justice for the poor.

In this Southern city the members of the Open Door reflect upon their lives together and the work they do, and they pray. In light of their own lives and work, the Bible, and Christian faith, they analyze how divisions and domination based upon class, race, gender, and sexuality have created and sustain a culture and social institutions that deny human dignity. They see that homelessness and prisons and executions are cultural and institutional expressions of these divisions and this domination. The community ministers to those injured because of class, race, gender or sexuality. It stands in opposition to the cultural convictions and institutional arrangements built upon these differences. The Open Door continues the tradition of Christian resistance with its insistence on the radical vision and practice of the Gospel that undercuts domination and oppression based on difference.

Its resistance is not only in the work of the community and its protests; it is in the very life of the community itself. I mentioned earlier the diversity in the community. A wide variety of people come to the Open Door to join in its life, work, and vision of the Reign of God. Some have experiences that echo in some way those of the founders of the community. They come to the Open Door uneasy with the "American dream." They have experienced in various ways how this dream is personally disturbing and harmful, how it is contrary to Christian faith, and how it demands complicity with oppression inconsistent with following Jesus. With this realization—this conversion to a more radical Christian discipleship—their previous lives as ministers, carpenters, teachers, nurses, truck drivers, students, or accountants are overturned. Seeking a new way of life based on the Gospel, they come to the Open Door.

From the start of the community, there have also been people from the streets and prisons who have come to the Open Door as a place to renew their lives. For example, Ralph Dukes stayed at the night shelter at Clifton that Ed, Murphy, Rob and Carolyn started, and he eventually came to move in with the community at 910 Ponce de Leon. The path of those like Ralph differs from those who join the Open Door with some degree of material prosperity and personal choice. The needs for a place to live and a community to support a break with their old way of life are more obvious and immediate for those persons who come to the Open Door from the streets and prisons. Homeless and living in the streets, or just out of prison, they are invited into the community. Of the many who have responded, some have stayed and become partners in the community, sharing in the leadership of the Open Door. Resurrected from the death of the streets and the prisons, they now share their new lives by aiding their brothers and sisters. Much of the variety and depth of the Open Door Community's life comes from the sharing of life by these members of the community from the streets and prisons with those members drawn from more materially prosperous backgrounds. And too, much of the suffering of the community over the years has come when persons, either from the streets and prisons or from other circumstances, have left the community. Especially difficult has been the departure of those whose addictions led them back to the streets.

One could tell the story of the Open Door Community in a number of different ways. In writing about the Open Door in the first version of this book, I relied on my own experience with the community from 1987-1990, on interviews, and on articles written by community members. I tried to give a sense of the people and the places that make up the community. For this version I draw again on that experience (and what I wrote). But I have also spent some significant time with the community (three months in the summer of 2003 and two additional months in the winter of 2005), conducted new interviews, and reviewed various written sources, including, of course, the community's newspaper *Hospitality*. With the community approaching its 25th anniversary it is time to bring the story into the present by weaving into the history the years since 1990.

I do not tell the story as a historian but rather as a Christian theologian and ethicist who believes that stories reveal the vision and the virtues of the Christian life. Thus, as with the first edition of this book, I hope to keep the focus on the people of the Open Door and to reflect upon what this story means for Christian discipleship. I continue to seek to weave together the number of smaller stories that have shaped the community over the past twenty-five years. Community members will tell how they came to the Open Door, why they have stayed or left, and the difficulties people face in living in such a place. These members and many of the people the community touches with its hospitality will tell what the Open Door means in their lives.

I hope that through these stories you will hear the community speak of its life together, its work, its prayer, and its protest. Please realize, too, that the separation of the stories into different chapters is artificial. It suggests a division in the life of the community between such things as the work of hospitality, worship, and activism. In reality, the community's life consists of overlapping circles, a circle formed for prayer, for meeting, for gathering to eat, for preparation to protest.

In the stories of community, I have continually sought to understand the vision of life held by the community and how that faithful vision is expressed in their shared life and work. I also continue to consider the place of the Open Door Community within Christianity and American society. Two questions were central in the first book and remain central in this edition. How does the Open Door offer a morally coherent alternative to the dominant values in American society? How does the community understand itself in relation to the Gospel as it is lived in the United States today? A third question also continues to tag along, and perhaps it grounds the concerns of the previous two—what does the Open Door say to us about being Christian disciples today?

I

COMING TOGETHER AT CLIFTON PRESBYTERIAN CHURCH

ON EACH SUNDAY AS EVENING DRAWS NEAR, the Open Door Community gathers for Eucharist. The dining room, where meals are served to homeless poor during the week, becomes the worship space. The long tables for meals are removed, and the chairs are circled around a small table set in the center of the room, upon which are placed the bread and the cup. Homeless people, who earlier in the week have partaken of the soup kitchen, the showers, the breakfast, and the foot clinic, are welcomed for worship. Volunteers, who have served at various times of the week, are also greeted. Everyone puts on name

tags, though most already know each other. As 5 P.M. nears, the chairs fill. Murphy Davis invites people to the first hymn. The voices of everyone gathered join with guitars, banjo, bass, drums, a piano, and Dick Rustay's trusty clarinet, a joyful noise is made unto the Lord. For the next several hours there is worship: prayers of the people, songs, readings, reflections, and finally bread is broken and passed, the cup is blessed and shared. The service ends with embraces, sharing the peace of Christ. The week's joys and sorrows, laughter and tears, are offered up to God, and the people gathered are renewed in the strength of the Lord for the work of the Lord. The promised Beloved Community is present as people of different races, social classes, genders, sexual orientations, nationalities, are joined into the one Body of Christ in the sharing of the bread of life and the cup of salvation. Then, it is time for dinner!

How do people come to form and sustain a Christian community where radical discipleship is practiced in the Spirit of Jesus through service to the poor and the work for justice? There is no one answer to that question. But stories such as that of the Open Door Community can help to illuminate the journey.

The Open Door gradually emerged out of a process that had its origins in the lives of two couples who met at Clifton Presbyterian Church, a small urban church in Atlanta. Ed Loring was the pastor of Clifton. Murphy Davis, his wife, was leading the Southern Prison Ministry, which had an office at the church. Rob and Carolyn Johnson joined the church in 1977. At the time Rob was working with a Methodist church program, "Meals on Wheels," that brought food to disabled and elderly "shut-ins." Carolyn was working with the Dekalb Community Council on Aging, in particular directing projects that helped low income senior citizens with repair of their homes.

These four people began a friendship that got its initial impetus from mutual interests and similarity in backgrounds. All four came from middle class families and entered adulthood in the 1960s. Ed, Murphy, and Carolyn were all raised in the South. And after moving to the South in 1967 to go to college, Rob also stayed in this region.

Coming of age as Southern whites, they saw how the legacy of slavery, the isolation of segregation, and years of discrimination, combined to impoverish blacks and create white fear and guilt. They listened as Martin Luther King, Jr., powerfully evoked a biblical message of liberation, redemption, and reconciliation, while also holding up American constitutional ideals in the call for civil rights. They saw how most white Christians opposed the Civil Rights Movement while it was endorsed by only a few. And as white Southern Christians they felt a responsibility to be involved as people of faith in this struggle for justice.

In varying degrees, all four sought to respond to the message of Dr. King and the Civil Rights Movement. Rob and Carolyn Johnson met each other while attending Florida Presbyterian College (now Eckerd). Following their graduation in

1971 they worked for three years in a Methodist social program that addressed racial problems in a transitional neighborhood in Greenville, South Carolina. As a college student in the early 1960s, Ed Loring was involved in black-white student dialogues held on campus. For Murphy Davis it was a summer away from the South, studying at the University of Colorado, that allowed her to meet with minority group prisoners and hear first hand of racial biases in sentencing and treatment. When she returned to the South, her eyes were opened to the racial dynamics of Southern prisons.

These experiences of living in the South, and their own initial efforts to respond to the message of King and others in the Civil Rights Movement, revealed to them the depth of resistance among white Americans to racial equality. They saw that civil rights legislation had brought some significant changes, but wealthy whites still held most institutional and cultural power. The three evils in American society that Dr. King had identified—racism, economic injustice, and militarism—remained.

In their own churches, they saw that despite the legal gains made by the Civil Rights Movement and efforts by a few progressive ministers, Sunday remained, as Dr. King said, "the most segregated day of the week." They knew Martin Luther King, Jr.'s prophetic denunciation of this racism in the white Christian churches. The contrast between the truth of Dr. King's message and the continuation of white church members' opposition to racial integration and economic justice left them dissatisfied. Most white churches, including their own, preached a Gospel that was applicable only in selective circumstances and social settings. In essence, this "white Gospel" applied to personal relationships, but not to public life. It was more concerned with swearing as an evil than with segregation. Most white churches focused on personal piety and individual moral purity. "Race mixing" violated purity. Personal salvation meant a privatized confession of faith in Jesus that was divorced from work for racial justice and the ending of segregation. Instead, for so many white church members, the Gospel's emphasis upon love and unity in Christ applied "spiritually" but had no social or public significance.

In addition to the Civil Rights Movement, Ed, Murphy, Carolyn and Rob were also significantly influenced by the second great social movement of the 1960s, the effort to end the Vietnam War. Here again Dr. King's message was influential, as were others who called for an end to this immoral war. For almost the entire time the four founders were in college or graduate school, campuses were places that fostered resistance to the war and made space for developing radical political thought.

Murphy, Ed, Rob, and Carolyn shared the view with growing numbers of students that the war was morally reprehensible and conducted by a government that could not be trusted. Further, they saw that until near the end of the war, mainline churches either stood silently by or endorsed the war effort. The massive firepower used, the defoliation of large areas of forest and cropland using Agent Orange, the creation of a huge refugee population, and the rising death toll on both sides indicated to students like these four that American power and technology had run amok. Like other students they were further alienated by the deceptions practiced at the highest levels of government. They saw themselves as having made the mistake of believing in the United States. For such students who were Christian, the failure of the churches to speak out against the war seemed akin to the failure of churches in the United States to speak out against slavery or the German churches to speak out against the Nazis.

During much of this time, Ed Loring was in graduate school, first earning a Master of Divinity degree at Columbia Theological Seminary in Atlanta, followed by doctoral studies, initially at Drew University and then at Vanderbilt. As a teaching assistant, he remained close to the issues of the student movement against the war. Murphy Davis participated in and helped coordinate demonstrations while she attended Mary Baldwin College. The school's proximity to several other colleges and to Washington, D.C. (just over an hour away) made this a particularly lively campus for anti-war activities. At Florida Presbyterian College, Rob and Carolyn Johnson met faculty who openly criticized the war effort and the government. Rob recalled intense discussions concerning the morality of the war and the possibilities of continuing resistance against the "establishment" after college. His own moral repugnance toward the war led him to apply for conscientious objector status on religious grounds. Granted his exemption, he did two years of alternative service.

During their years in school, all four of them became familiar with a "New Left" analysis of American society that also resonated with Dr. King's views. New Left theorists and activists analyzed the war as part of larger moral and institutional faults in American life. They saw the government's military involvement in Vietnam as indicative of an American society increasingly dominated by an ethic of efficiency and profits. As Dr. King had said in "Beyond Vietnam," his speech at Riverside Church on April 4, 1967, the nation needed a "radical revolution of values" to "rapidly shift from a thing-oriented society to a person-oriented society. When machines and computers, profit motives and property rights, are considered more important than people, the giant triplets of racism, extreme materialism, and militarism are incapable of being conquered." Like Dr. King, the New Left saw the massive bombings and the use of Agent Orange in Vietnam, the stockpiling of nuclear weapons, the problems of air and water pollution, and inner city poverty as symptoms of a technological and economic system intent on profit instead of human good. The worship of technology prevented ethical considerations of its impact on human lives. Bureaucratic political and corporate structures kept responsibility for this suffering dispersed and unacknowledged. Dr. King pointed to these realities in his "Beyond Vietnam" speech when he warned of those who "possess power without compassion, might without morality, and strength without sight."

The New Left called for a revival of "participatory democracy" in which a sense of moral community and of the cooperative dimension of human nature could be recovered. The social ideals of the New Left were to be put into practice by communities working and organizing with the poor. These communities would develop capabilities for tackling local issues that would expose and seek to transform the larger structural faults in American society. Dr. King's "Poor People's Campaign" was to initiate a nonviolent revolution in which the political and economic institutions of this nation would be put into the service of the people, rather than serve the interests of the elite.

Gradually, Rob, Carolyn, Ed, and Murphy became aware of some Christians who were combining elements of this "New Left" analysis with faith convictions, and this resonated with their knowledge of Dr. King. In their work at the Methodist social program in Greenville, Rob and Carolyn Johnson encountered church people committed to this New Left critique. These people believed the New Left critique and vision provided a helpful social analysis compatible with the Christian vision of God's reign as announced and enacted by Jesus. Murphy Davis and Ed Loring were attracted in their studies to the work of New Left historians, such as Howard Zinn, who analyzed the history of the United States from the perspective of those harmed and oppressed in the development of the nation. They began to make connections on the academic level between New Left ideas and Anabaptist traditions in Protestantism, along with Dr. King's theology and activism.

By the early 1970s, all four of them were reading the "Post-American," a paper published by leftist evangelicals such as Jim Wallis, initially united by their faith-based resistance to the Vietnam War. Those publishing this paper later began the Sojourners Community located in Washington, D.C., where they engaged in social protest and ministry with the poor. The paper became a magazine sharing the same name as the community. Such communities and their publications became gathering places for ideas and practices regarding how Christian faith could provide a more enduring ground for social critique and activism than the secular ideologies evident in the anti-war movement and the New Left.

Among these Christian activists there was a concern that the critique of the New Left was too connected with an Enlightenment belief in the perfectibility of human community. The gathering movement of Christian activists began to see that this optimism needed to be balanced by a more sober understanding of human nature, one that recognized human weaknesses and failure, in a word, sin. And with this sobriety there was need for a deeper sustaining spirit that would not be discouraged in the face of difficulty. Faith resources were needed "for the long haul." Like others, Rob, Carolyn, Murphy and Ed struggled with these issues as they sought to bring together their faith convictions and the social analysis offered by the New Left. They were seeking a coherent vision of faith and community life that could ground their social commitments and activism.

In this search, both couples had attempted to form intentional communities before they met at Clifton. Both experiments ended rather quickly. The mutuality and cooperative feeling promised by New Left writings folded under the real pressures and conflicts of community life. Although there were some Christian motivations behind the forming of both communities, the expectation was community would nurture each member's emotional life. Service in the context of responding to the call of the Gospel had not been central. These experiences made each couple skeptical of forming a community without giving it some purpose beyond its own existence.

Given their religious backgrounds, each of the founders also recognized in mainline Protestantism some resources for developing their social activism grounded in a faith community. Ed Loring was raised a Southern Baptist. In his youth he heard his pastor Carlyle Marney preach a "social gospel" that was not common within this conservative Southern denomination. The social gospel movement in American Protestantism had first emerged in response to social problems caused by industrialization in the United States, primarily in the North. Walter Rauschenbusch, one of its leading theological proponents, summed up its spirit as a combining of the Gospel with efforts for social justice for the poor through a "democratization" of economic life. Martin Luther King, Jr., educated in a Northern predominately white seminary (Crozer) and graduate school (Boston University), was profoundly affected by the ideals of the social gospel as he brought together Christian faith with work for social justice. For him, the social gospel echoed the best traditions of the Black Church in terms of resistance to social evil and transformation of members for involvement in social change.

Ed was further exposed to the social gospel during his studies at Columbia Theological Seminary. Neely McCarter, one of Ed's professors was especially influential. Ed began to see more promise for continuing in this social gospel approach in the Presbyterian Church than in his own Southern Baptist tradition. In 1964, at age twenty-four he became a Presbyterian. In 1971, Ed completed his Ph.D. coursework at Vanderbilt and returned to Columbia to teach church history while working on his dissertation. In that same year he was ordained a Presbyterian minister.

Unlike Ed, Murphy was raised in the Presbyterian Church. Her father was a Presbyterian minister who along with her mother encouraged interest in the social issues of the day. Murphy's interest in the church and ministry had been strengthened during a year she spent in Brazil between high school and college (1966–1967). There she experienced an awakened social consciousness from seeing so much poverty and from experiencing the warm, expressive, fervent Brazilian Presbyterianism so unlike the formal Presbyterian style of worship in which she grew up. Her social consciousness was further nourished during her college days of anti-war protest, and through her contact with prisoners while studying in Denver. After earning her Master's of Divinity degree from Columbia in 1976, she was ordained a Presbyterian minister.

Carolyn Johnson and Rob Johnson were raised in the Presbyterian Church. Like Murphy, Rob's father was also a Presbyterian minister. As a minister, Rob's father had been active in civil rights issues in New Castle, Delaware, where Rob's family lived. Rob's mother (like Ed's) was a Head Start teacher. Through both of his parents Rob had gained some sense of the race and class dynamics that work to impoverish people. Carolyn's parents were both very active in their Presbyterian Church in Oak Ridge, Tennessee. The church was an island for progressive thinking and the minister encouraged support for the civil rights movement. Carolyn in her last year of high school did special studies on African American history and the civil rights movement. Encouraged to be active in church life while growing up, Carolyn and Rob gravitated toward church work following college.

Following their work in the Methodist social program at Greenville, they became active in the Wesley Center while they were graduate students at the University of Georgia from 1974 to 1977. When they moved to Atlanta, Rob began his work with the Methodist church's "Meals on Wheels" program, and Carolyn began work with elderly persons. Additionally, Rob and Carolyn participated in a "house church" in Marietta, Georgia (a northern suburb of Atlanta), as part of their ongoing search for a faith community that combined a closely-knit community with social concern.

Though all four found some resources in mainline Protestantism for faith-based activism, their experiences and education also made them increasingly aware that this mainline Protestantism could only go so far in its criticism of, and resistance to, the dominant American culture. Mainline Protestantism was especially limited in that it continued to reflect social divisions along racial and class lines. In their own experience, they saw that mainline churches mustered only timid criticisms of the dominant values in American culture. The churches were in Dr. King's words, "more tail-lights than headlights" in American society. These mainline churches had rarely, or reluctantly, questioned the wars of the United States. Their response to how the poor were neglected in a society that defined success through the over-consumption of goods, or how the American economic and political systems militated against the vulnerable, consisted more of charity than justice.

On race, the mainline churches had divided over slavery, and had a mixed record of support for civil rights. Typically the national office or perhaps minister (as was the case with each of the founders) of a mainline church was more progressive than the people in the pews, and most ministers were generally unwilling to challenge their congregations too much. The four founders sensed that the faith in these churches was more focused on individual salvation and the Gospel message trimmed to create a faith devoid of much political or economic import. Too often congregations were like private clubs, places of refuge where people of a certain race and class met to escape the unpleasantness of the world. The four founders grew restive with a church largely comfortable with the role American society had given it: protector of private morality and place of gathering for people of the same income, lifestyle, and race.

During their three years in Greenville, Rob and Carolyn were increasingly frustrated by the attitude of people within the local church. Rob relates that he and Carolyn kept "finding ourselves the token do-gooders paid by the church to do this social work." The people of the church did not want to be personally involved with the poor. They were satisfied to give money so that others could "manage" those problems. This approach kept members of the congregation distant from the poor. Members of the church seemed to think that the best thing to do with the poor was to leave them in the hands of experts, such as Rob and Carolyn were perceived to be, and mind one's own business. The poor were objects of charity rather than persons who in justice should be empowered to fully participate in the life of the community.

This attitude stood in direct opposition to Rob and Carolyn's convictions formed by their Christian faith and increasingly influenced by the New Left critique, Dr. King, and activist Christians. They saw personal involvement with the poor and systemic change as inseparable components of Christian life and social action. Christian faith should lead to charity for those in need, but it also demanded work to end the injustice which caused need. To separate charity and justice, the personal and the public dimensions of life, seemed biblically and morally incoherent.

Their experience at Greenville initiated in them a process of alienation from the institutional church. They saw that most of their social activist friends were not churchgoers. Among these friends were people active in the women's movement who were helping organize NOW chapters. Feminism, the third social movement of the 1960s, was seen as an important piece of the overall commitment to human liberation they saw as central to the Gospel. Before visiting Clifton Presbyterian

Church in late 1977, Carolyn and Rob had almost despaired of finding a church that brought together Christian faith and worship with a liberal to leftist social vision and a commitment to feminism.

While Rob and Carolyn were struggling to make sense of their faith and their experiences of social activism, Ed and Murphy were also attempting to bring together their beliefs and social convictions. Initially this struggle was focused on Ed's teaching at Columbia Seminary. There he began to personally experience what he saw as the cultural captivity of American churches expressed in the tendency to reduce Christian ethics to an individualistic moralism. This reduction left the public spheres of politics and economics to function autonomously following their own laws of cost and efficiency. Meanwhile, the private spheres of family and church would safeguard a private morality of love. As a professor of church history and ethics at Columbia, Ed came into conflict with this moralism and its refusal to confront the values of the public sphere.

He had taught there for four years when his first marriage ended in divorce. In the spring of 1975 Ed planned to marry for a second time. Many of the Columbia faculty were already antagonistic towards Ed because of his fiery personality and leftist political convictions. He intended in his teaching "to lead people to make choices about life; to influence people to make choices about the left." He summed up his approach at this time as "anti-capitalist, anti–North American, with some commitment to a liberal Jesus." The more conservative and staid members of the faculty saw this as an attack on their vision of Christian life and ministry. It went directly against their more benign view of America as well as against their sense that religion should keep its distance from political issues. Ed's divorce from his wife with whom he had had two children, and then his marriage to Murphy Davis, a younger former Columbia student, who was also divorced, only further violated their

CLIFTON PRESBYTERIAN CHURCH, LATE 1970S

sense of moral propriety. Out of these conflicts came the decision by Columbia not to renew Ed's contract.

The Atlanta Presbytery found a position for Ed in which they hoped he and the controversy at Columbia could be quietly forgotten: Clifton Presbyterian Church in Atlanta. Bill Adams of the Presbytery told Ed, "Clifton is a dying church. All you have to do is preach on Sunday, visit folks when they go to the hospital, and don't worry if the church closes while you're there. It's been dying for a long time." It was a place no one wanted to pastor—a dead end for anyone with eyes on a pastoral career. Ed, angry and hurt by what had happened at Columbia, saw it as a temporary position. It would allow him time to finish writing his Ph.D. dissertation, and provide some income and a place to live while Murphy went through her doctoral program at Emory. They planned on staying at Clifton for, at most, three years, and then with Ph.D.'s in hand, they hoped to leave and begin comfortable lives as New-Left church historians at some denominational college, preferably in the mountains. But then a Bible study began to change their lives. And when

Rob and Carolyn joined Clifton and the Bible study, the two couples began talk about their experiences and their hopes and dreams for Christian life. Not only did a friendship grow, so too did their sense of a deeper calling to Christian discipleship and the possibilities for a transformed church life.

© BILL HORRISBERGER

BIBLE STUDY AT CLIFTON PRESBYTERIAN CHURCH, LATE 1970S

2

GROWING IN DISCIPLESHIP

BEFORE ROB AND CAROLYN HAD ARRIVED AT CLIFTON, a member of the congregation asked Ed to begin a Sunday evening Bible study. The focus of the study was not scholarly exegesis. Ed and Murphy's theological training had emphasized study of the Bible using the method of historical criticism. But in their experience, such a method seemed mostly an intellectual exercise unconnected with their daily life or that of the congregation at Clifton. Something more was needed to give biblical studies transformative power within daily life. Ed and Murphy realized that if the Bible was to speak with theological and moral authority, they had to personally grapple with the text within the context of their lives. What the Bible proclaimed about God and human life had to be taken seriously by allowing it to claim the way they lived. They had to enter the biblical world and let biblical reality shape their lives. Their world had to be put into question by God's word in the Bible.

The Bible study gathered to ask "What does this passage mean for us in our lives?" The push to start with this question came from two sources, liberation theology and "biblical realism." Liberation theology was then emerging in Latin America, and "biblical realism" was being popularized by a Mennonite theologian, John Howard Yoder, in his book, *The Politics of Jesus.* "Biblical realism" according to Yoder, insisted that there are certain characteristics of the biblical vision "which refuse to be pushed into the mold of any one contemporary world view, but which stand in creative tension with the cultural functions of our age or perhaps any age." As developed by Yoder and others, this biblical interpretation attends to the social and political dimensions of Jesus' life and teaching, rather than dismissing them as "eschatological" in the sense of "otherworldly."

Liberation theology urged that theology, including biblical studies, has to emerge from the lived experiences of the people, especially the poor and their struggle for liberation. The interpretive method of liberation theology helped the Bible study at Clifton to focus around two principles and two related questions. First, the Bible must be read for its liberating message. How does this passage speak to the struggle for human freedom? Second, there must be dialogue between the Bible's historical context and the context of the readers. How does the Bible's addressing of its context relate to the context of those seeking to participate in the struggle for human freedom?

Combining these two approaches of biblical realism and liberation theology, those in the Bible study began to raise questions about the faithfulness of the congregation to the

Gospel. They began to consider in what ways Jesus' life and teachings might be incompatible with the realities of American society, might challenge mainline Protestantism, and might challenge their community of faith.

In this Bible study, Ed and Murphy were discerning a more profound basis for the social critique they had learned in the 1960s. The vision of life they began to discover in the Bible struck them as more compelling, comprehensive and consistent than what the New Left had offered. It brought them into further study of Martin Luther King, Jr.'s theological and moral convictions which had been so powerful in the Civil Rights and Peace Movements. Meanwhile, the Bible study continued to challenge them to wrestle with the meaning of the Bible in the context of the people and events at Clifton.

Ed and Murphy's rediscovery of the Bible and black liberation struggles as a crucial resource for their lives began to undermine their academic plans. Their dream of a safe activism as liberal and critical academics started to seem self-centered and irrelevant. Ed began to find being pastor of this small church was more enlivening than he had thought possible. He found his academic theological work could no longer compare with his pastoral ministry. Murphy, too, was finding shortcomings in her studies at Emory. She increasingly experienced the academic process as individualistic and overly focused on competition between students. Her experiences were in sharp contrast to not only what she was learning in the Bible, but also to her deepening feminist perspective. With regard to the latter, in the summers of 1974 and 1975 Murphy participated in the Project for Women in Theological Education held at Grailville, Ohio. She felt these experiences were life-giving, while her graduate studies were deadening. Murphy recalls that, "At Grailville education was not the pure pursuit of knowledge, but included the building of the human person, and building relationships. At Emory we found it impossible to figure out how to work together. The process made everyone individualistic. You were to work alone and present your findings."

Murphy and Ed were searching for a Christian life that was more biblically faithful, more communal, less individualistic, and more critical of American materialism, racism, and militarism. They were seeing too much of American Christianity as a kind spiritualized and individualized religion that was neither competent nor inclined to criticize dominant economic or political life. In the Bible study, Murphy and Ed were finding the liberating God of the Bible who went far beyond feeling good about being saved and being morally good on an individual level. Salvation meant liberation from sin and this meant a personal transformation that placed persons in a shared struggle with the poor and oppressed for justice.

As these insights began to enter into the lives of Murphy, Ed and some of the other participants in the Bible study, they began to make changes in several areas of congregational life at Clifton. Sunday worship was transformed. Since worship in the Bible involved the whole person, binding the community together through the Word and ritual action, a more emotional and tactile style of worship reflecting Black Church influences developed at Clifton. The community began celebrating the Lord's Supper more frequently. They shared their concerns with one another in the context of worship, held hands during the Lord's Prayer, and embraced at the "kiss of peace." They rearranged the sanctuary so that the community could sit in semi-circles around the pulpit, and the pulpit itself was placed on floor level. Music in worship became more lively. Murphy recalls that the piano tuner said the piano at Clifton was "the only Presbyterian one in town to have the pedals stomped off." Pastoral leadership came not from above, but from collaboration with the congregation. Further, the New Testament passage from Galatians 3:28 that allowed for no hierarchy between male and female in Christ led to active roles for women in worship and the use of inclusive language.

Worship at Clifton also sought to embody the biblical insistence (especially evident in Jesus and the prophets) on the connection between worship and the practice of social justice in the lives of the participants. Worship which made people feel good but did not move them to seek justice in their way of life and in society was offensive to God. Worship was to be the basis for community action. In response to the Word and Eucharist, people were to be empowered to bring their faith into every sphere of life, serve others, and seek justice. A number of the members of this small congregation of about thirty people earnestly sought to express these convictions. By late 1976 the church was sponsoring social programs connecting worship to service. In addition to opening a food pantry for low-income neighbors, the church began to offer several meals each week and a weekly evening of recreation for youth from McLendon Gardens, a nearby low-income housing project. Another area of social involvement was soon added as the congregation offered support for Murphy's growing ministry with prisoners.

This ministry had emerged when Murphy was confronted with an issue that compelled her attention in a way graduate studies never could. In July 1976, the Supreme Court upheld the constitutionality of the newly revised Georgia death penalty law. Murphy and Ed were already involved with Georgia Christians Against the Death Penalty, a group Ed had helped to start. This was one of a number of small groups in Georgia that came together to protest the Supreme Court decision and to seek to change the law. In November 1976, Murphy and Ed traveled to Macon with their close friend Austin Ford for a meeting of this group. There they met and listened to the mothers of several death row prisoners, including Betty George, Marian Butler, and Viva Lamb. Murphy recalls that Viva Lamb's address was especially powerful:

> Viva very simply described the pain and ostracism and that whole level of grief—the further victimization—that was created by the death penalty. Somebody had been victimized by the murder, and now a whole new set of victims was created as they waited for their family member on death row to die.

Hearing these women speak rekindled Murphy's concern for prisoners which she had first felt as a college student. She sensed that the Bible study and her dissatisfaction with graduate studies had been training her ears to hear a call from God to serve people who were poor and oppressed. Now the call became defined in the form of ministry with prisoners, especially prisoners on death row. After a year and a half of graduate studies at Emory University, Murphy decided that life in a study carrel was not for her. She quit graduate school and began to search for a way to follow the call she heard.

She did not have to search long. In early January 1977, Joe Ingle of the Southern Coalition on Prisons hired Murphy to organize in Atlanta a national demonstration against the death penalty. The "Witness Against Executions" was scheduled for Easter weekend of that year. Clifton supplied office space for Murphy and she went to work. A year and a half before, the church had been written off as dead. Now it became the meeting place for nationally known foes of the death penalty, for the planning of demonstration strategy, and for the training of marshals for the march. Some 3,000 people from around the United States came to participate in the demonstration which gathered national media attention.

Following this mass protest, Murphy decided to continue her advocacy for prisoners and her work against the death penalty. She formed the Southern Prison Ministry Georgia office and began organizing prison visits for the relatives of prisoners who did not have the means to make the five-hour drive from

PHOTOGRAPHS © CALVIN KIMBROUGH

MURPHY DAVIS (RIGHT) SPEAKS AT THE "WITNESS AGAINST EXECUTIONS," STATE CAPITOL, ATLANTA, APRIL 1977

Atlanta to the state prison, located in Reidsville. By 1978, this had become a monthly excursion which, as Murphy described it, meant mothers jammed into an old blue van, "going to visit their sons, with huge baskets filled with fried chicken and potato salad." As Murphy, Ed, and a few other members of the congregation drove on these trips, they began to learn first-hand about poverty, prison sentences made longer because of one's race, and the depth of faith and hope among these women and their loved ones in prison. This experience began to enter into and shape their biblical interpretation and their lives.

Among those who became involved with the Bible study and ministry with the Clifton congregation were Carolyn and

Rob Johnson. In late 1977, at a gathering of the Atlanta Presbytery Task Force on Hunger, Ed and Rob met. Ed invited Rob to worship at Clifton. Rob and Carolyn responded to the invitation and found the kind of church they had long sought. Carolyn recalled that Clifton immediately felt different from all their previous church experiences: "We felt at home the first time we were at Clifton. There was a focus on social justice issues and a very spiritual, worshipful environment. Also the language was inclusive. We'd never hoped in terms of a church to find all three of those things." The more lively worship combined with social activism was attracting Christians from various denominations who shared varying degrees of disaffection with mainline churches and American society.

For Ed, Murphy, and now Rob and Carolyn, Clifton was providing the context for a theological deepening and expanding of the social critique they had formed in the 1960s. They became more aware of the biblical and African American Church sources for Martin Luther King Jr.'s work in the Civil Rights and Peace Movements. This combination of fervent communal spirituality and social action was a model they hoped to emulate at Clifton. But they soon discovered they could only take this model so far within a traditional denominational setting.

The Bible study remained the catalyst for personal and congregational transformation at Clifton. This became somewhat problematic, however, since the whole congregation did not participate in the study itself. Those who gathered on Sunday evenings tended to be the more committed members of the church, and more critical of mainline churches and the United States. Rob described the Bible study as consisting of "people who shared some real skepticism about the mainline church. It had basically been co-opted by the culture and couldn't be relied upon to interpret what was going on in America." The people in the Bible study had a "shared value that society needs to change and religious people should be about that." The interaction of biblical study with political convictions led not only to critiques of American society and mainline religion, but also to criticism of the church at Clifton. After a while, this criticism began to take aim at the social ministry of the congregation.

Both the suppers and recreation night program and the prison ministry were part-time endeavors for the congregation and, like the Bible study, not everyone in the church participated. Even for those who did participate, their lives away from the church still generally followed the patterns of American society. Those in the Bible study were finding a biblical call for obedience to God in all areas of life. A passage from Isaiah 58 that called for sharing bread with the hungry, shelter with the homeless and liberating justice was becoming particularly important in their discernment. How could this call be lived with an institutional and ethical fragmentation in which life was divided into the different contexts of work, family, church, and politics and their differing moral demands?

Facing the tensions caused by this fragmentation, the issue of the mission of the congregation at Clifton began to sharpen. Especially among those in the Bible study there was a growing sense of dissatisfaction with the direction of the suppers and recreation night. It was requiring more crowd control of rambunctious youngsters, and offered little chance for the personal relationships the people of the church had hoped to form with the youth and their families. It was more care taking than mutual transformation. The prison ministry, on the other hand, was too forbidding for most, and was a small operation not requiring a significant commitment from the congregation. Essentially the church provided space and moral support for this ministry. With these issues in the forefront, a decision came from the Sunday evening Bible study to do an internal study of the congregation regarding Clifton's mission.

Rob Johnson was placed in charge of the study. He had done a similar mission exploration while working with churches in Greenville, South Carolina. The study at Clifton took the form of Wednesday night meetings in which a small group gathered around the questions: "What are the problems in Atlanta, or in our neighborhood, and what are the possible responses of our church?" After a month of such meetings, a serious split in the congregation over the question of mission became evident.

On the one hand, some members wanted the church to focus inward. The mission of the church was conceived as building up fellowship among the members of the congregation. Reflecting a more privatized view of religious life, this group saw the church primarily as a refuge from the turbulence and competitiveness of the world. Given the immensity of social problems and their intractable nature, it was best to turn inward and create a community of support where one felt safe and secure. On the other hand, some wanted a church turned outward. They saw the church as essentially a base for actions to promote social justice. Christians should be social activists. This group had numerous ideas about what the church at Clifton should do, but was unable to reach a consensus on any one of them.

At this point the mission study at Clifton stalled. The very model of the church held by Ed, Murphy, Rob, Carolyn, and others in the congregation, who sought to combine a more wholistic spirituality and social action, was now being questioned. The study had unearthed tensions in the congregation over this vision and its practice. It revealed that the congregation could not decide what type of life it hoped to foster. It appeared as if the congregation's division would prevent any fundamental alteration of its life.

Instead of forcing the issue, the leaders of the study decided they needed to discern what the split in the congregation meant for the church and for the possibilities of Christian life in American society. Could intense spirituality and an emphasis on community be joined with social activism? Or must these remain separate in a society where people choose to participate in the church as it fits their needs and schedules?

To examine and reflect upon these questions, a small group continued to meet on Wednesday nights after the mission study ended. This group consistently included the four eventual founders of the Open Door—Ed, Murphy, Carolyn, and Rob. They gathered to share a meal, read scripture, pray, and also to discuss articles about poverty and Christian discipleship drawn from sources such as *Sojourners,* a magazine published by the Sojourners' community in Washington, D.C. They still hoped to somehow combine, in their lives and in the congregation, intensity of spirit with social action.

Sojourners presented them with examples of Christian communities that seemed to have these characteristics. Such communities served the poor and went beyond the denominational model of church life. In alternative Christian communities, a biblical ethic could be practiced in all facets of life. To Rob, Carolyn, Murphy, and Ed, this type of life now appeared as the best possible resource for breaking with their experience of an ineffectual congregational model trying to address both Christian community and social ministry.

With this realization growing among the group, one question came to be central: "God, what will you have us do?" As the meetings continued into the fall of 1978, there was, according to Rob, "a growing clarity that something important about the Gospel was the issue of being in proximity with the poor." Jesus had habitually associated with the outcasts, the marginalized, the poor of the land. His example and words were taken as normative. The consensus grew that "God was calling us to serve the poor and to live our lives based on the Scriptures." Ed put it this way: "We recognized that the call to serve God is the call to serve the poor." With this emphasis on service to the poor, the vision of life that had its inception in the Sunday night Bible study became sharper. An important second step toward the formation of the Open Door Community was now underway.

Their discussions began to center on what form this service to and solidarity with the poor should take. They were convinced that to be faithful to the story of Jesus, their service must come through personal and sustained involvement with the lives of the poor. It would not be enough to be part-time servants. They now noticed that "in our weekly Bible study, readings, and prayers with others at Clifton, we kept sensing an out-of-our-control drive to break a 'barrier between ourselves and the poor.'" This barrier they felt was being built "out of our own heads that told us to be realistic, and our own fears and uncertainties [that] kept us from the poor." Their middle class value of competitive individualism had erected a wall of judgment between them and the poor. To be poor meant one had failed as a human being. Further, residential segregation by wealth and race, and church life, militated against dismantling that wall. How would they be able to break down that wall within their own lives, and in the life of the Clifton congregation?

The scriptures, it appeared to them, were fairly clear about how people should live in obedient response to God. Two passages, one from the Old Testament and one from the New, emerged as especially formative in their lives. The first was Isaiah 58:6–7: "The kind of fasting I want is this: remove the chains of oppression and the yoke of injustice, and let the oppressed go free. Share your food with the hungry and open your homes to the homeless poor. Give clothes to those who have nothing to wear, and do not refuse to help your own relatives." As Murphy later noted, "You know that when we begin to share food with each other and open the table to strangers, the Spirit starts to move into our lives in unexpected ways." The second passage, Matthew 25:31–46, told of the last judgment in which those who served the hungry, the thirsty, the naked and the imprisoned were saved. This passage had long been influential in Christian groups that sought social and ecclesiastical reform or radical change, and now it once again shaped the moral vision of Murphy, Ed, Rob, and Carolyn. Murphy found that Matthew 25 had provided:

> . . . the most consistent light for us. . . . The whole vision that is given to us is that in the people among us now who are marginalized in any way—the hungry, the stranger, the naked, the prisoner—in their sufferings we come to understand the sufferings of Christ. Therefore at the heart of the Gospel is the mandate in Matthew 25. It is not only clear, it is harsh. If you do this, feed the hungry, welcome the stranger, clothe the naked, visit the prisoner, you're welcome into heaven. If you don't, you're going to hell. It's very stark and very clear. Do you spend your life with those who accumulate, or do you spend your life with those who are always on the outside and always suffering?

By January 1979, Murphy, Ed, Carolyn, and Rob were growing in the conviction that to be with those who were marginalized and suffering was necessary for Christian life and community. Part-time acts of charity done out of one's abundance and at one's convenience were no longer sufficient. Carolyn Johnson summarized their thinking at this point:

> It didn't make sense to be studying the Gospel and worshipping without trying to live a lifestyle that was compatible, as we saw it, with the Gospel. Ministry with the poor and oppressed was very much at the heart of

> what we were studying. We thought it was time to get involved with actually doing something.

The Bible study had led them to see God's activity on behalf of the enslaved, the poor, and the powerless. In these actions, God revealed God's liberating intent for human life and called upon humans to manifest it in every sphere. How could they live this biblical call to liberation at Clifton? The Southern Prison Ministry began by Murphy seemed a partial answer, but it was not enough. The very nature of prison ministry made for limited visits and time with prisoners. They could not go and live in the prisons. They believed that the Gospel called them to a more continuous, daily, and personal presence with the poor. They wanted to bring together their lives lived in response to the Gospel with lives lived in solidarity with the poor. They wanted to affirm the dignity of the poor and their membership in the human community. But they wondered how they might do this. How could they embody in their lives this wholistic biblical life?

3

OPENING THE NIGHT SHELTER AT CLIFTON

THERE WAS NO EASY ANSWER TO THE QUESTION ED, Murphy, Rob and Carolyn now faced. How would they respond to the biblical call to wholeness that emerged from their Bible study? A number of events began to move them toward responding with a radical change in their lives.

In January 1979, Murphy and Ed went to New York for a meeting related to the prison ministry. While in New York, they decided to visit Maryhouse, a Catholic Worker Movement house of hospitality for homeless persons. They met with the people who lived and worked at Maryhouse, and were moved by the warm and accepting hospitality offered to homeless people there. Mike Harank from the community advised them, "Let all your work be rooted in love, and stay small." As they left they were given a copy of Dorothy Day's autobiography, *The Long Loneliness.* Ed began to read it on the train ride back to Atlanta.

At this time, Ed and Murphy knew very little about Dorothy Day, the woman who along with Peter Maurin, had started the Catholic Worker Movement during the Great Depression of the 1930s. To this point they had become familiar with Sojourners and some of liberation theology, but had not heard much about the Catholic Worker or Dorothy Day. But as Ed read, he found much in Dorothy Day's life with which he could identify. She had lived a Bohemian lifestyle when young. She was an intellectual and a radical. She had joyfully, but also painfully, moved toward conversion. Her joy was in the birth of her child and a growing sense of the gracious presence of God in her life. Her pain was that in joining the church she not only lost many of her friends, but also the man she had lived with who was the father of her child. In her conversion, she became increasingly close to the poor, eventually joining with Peter Maurin to open a house of hospitality where the poor could find shelter, food, and welcome without questions or judgment. In the soup kitchens and social activism of the Catholic Worker Movement houses of hospitality, in their common life sustained by the Gospel and shared with the poor, Ed saw a possible response to the call he and Murphy, Carolyn and Rob were hearing in their Bible study and prayer. He thought this coming together of their searching and the work of hospitality portrayed in the Catholic Worker Movement pointed to "a movement of the Spirit."

He and Murphy began to share their reading of *The Long Loneliness* with each other. They began to see what this call of hospitality would require of them. It was an emotional trip back to Atlanta. Tears were shed, both out of joy for the possibility of work with the poor now presented them, and out of fear for what that might mean for their lives. Upon their return, Murphy and Ed quickly shared with Rob and Carolyn the enthusiasm they had felt about the call to hospitality they had heard at Maryhouse and through Dorothy Day's life story. Together they began to explore how they might do this work with the homeless in Atlanta.

As they investigated homelessness in Atlanta, they found a political and business elite that said the numbers of homeless in the city were insignificant. Homelessness, this elite held, was not worth addressing except with police action to keep the "vagrants" away from certain areas. The stereotype of the street person as a skid row bum drunk on cheap wine was strong and officially supported. Business and political leaders in the city claimed that the Salvation Army and the Union Mission, and when necessary jail, offered all that was needed for these dregs of society.

Yet in talking with people from the Salvation Army, the Union Mission, and with homeless people, they quickly discovered a different reality. The number of homeless persons in Atlanta was rapidly increasing, and among them were more and more African-Americans. The demeaning stereotype of worthless bum offered by business and political leaders covered up a more complex reality. Among the homeless were workers broken by years of hard manual labor; people forced into the streets by the destruction of low income housing; former textile mill workers and farmers who had come to the city looking for work, found none, and rapidly depleted their savings; Vietnam veterans who had not made the adjustment back to civilian life; mentally ill people who had been de-institutionalized; persons struggling with substance abuse; and hundreds of others, each with their own story of how they ended up on the streets. They learned that in 1979 an estimated two thousand people were homeless in Atlanta. The Salvation Army had fourteen beds for these people, and offered one free night every six months. The Union Mission offered additional space but still an inadequate number of beds, and allowed only three free nights per lifetime. These two institutions provided the only shelter available for the homeless in the city of Atlanta.

The more they learned, the more Murphy, Ed, Carolyn, and Rob became convinced that the most immediate need among homeless people was shelter. They considered how they might meet that need at Clifton. Starting a shelter, they decided, would be the way they could respond to the call discerned in their Bible study and prayer. This shelter would involve them personally with the homeless. The church could be opened as a sanctuary for homeless persons to share a meal, stay the night, shower, and get a change of clothes. Yet as they reflected further on this plan, they began to waver.

Opening a shelter at Clifton "just wasn't practical" at this time. Murphy and Carolyn were pregnant (Carolyn would give birth to Christina on May 3rd, two months premature); Rob needed back surgery; and the space at Clifton seemed too small for a shelter. It could hold, at most, twenty or thirty people for a night. It was time, they thought, to be realistic in responding to this biblical call to serve the poor. Considering all the facts, and seeing the strain it would put on them and the church, their enthusiasm dwindled and they concluded it would be best to "study the issue of homelessness and a shelter at Clifton for another year." "We rationalized," said Ed.

In August 1979, as part of their ongoing study, they invited Mitch Snyder from the Community for Creative Nonviolence (CCNV) in Washington, D.C. to come and speak to the congregation at Clifton about homelessness. Snyder was a former convict who had converted in prison where he had met Father Daniel Berrigan who was there for burning draft files at a draft board in Catonsville, Maryland. Snyder had founded CCNV along with other Christian activists and he had become a moral authority in the lives of many Christians who, like Ed, Murphy, Rob, and Carolyn, sought to combine Christian faith with a radical analysis of American society and a life with the poor.

His reputation among Christian activists had spread widely since he and others in CCNV had occupied the National Visitors Center in Washington, D.C., and used the empty building as a shelter for the homeless. The Department of the Interior agreed after negotiations to temporarily allow this use as an "experiment." When it was decided that the shelter had become an embarrassment to the city it was forcibly closed down. Snyder and others from his community were arrested. The CCNV, in addition to its soup kitchen and shelter, engaged in a number of public demonstrations in which they actively confronted city and church officials with the injustice of homelessness. Community life in CCNV was described by its members as "a blending of the elements of spirituality, direct service, resistance, constructive action, and the personal integration of justice."

Ed and Murphy picked Snyder up at the airport on Saturday night. He would speak at worship the following morning. Ed expected Snyder "to give us some little moral homily on how the poor need us, and next year we would have a shelter if we really tried hard." Instead, Snyder stood in the pulpit Sunday morning and told the congregation that there were people suffering and dying from homelessness in the city of Atlanta. If they were really Christians, Snyder bluntly said, they must respond to that injustice and that death. "You have this room at Clifton, you have a bathroom, you have resources. It would be immoral," he thundered, "if you did not open the doors this fall to the homeless poor of this city. There are thousands out there that need you, and this space belongs to them in justice." To put it mildly, the directness of Snyder's talk unsettled those who heard it. The tone was not soothing and the strong words of judgment made folks quite uncomfortable.

Snyder's radical preaching had gone beyond the kind of safe activism that was polite and limited to working through the appropriate channels and with appropriate decorum. Snyder presented the more threatening task of challenging the very system that produced homelessness and poverty. Homelessness, Synder claimed, was a symptom of a deeper systemic ill: a society based on isolation, competition, and self-interest could not lead to a community in which human dignity was affirmed. If Christians accepted this system, even if they practiced charity, they remained complicit in the social injustice perpetrated on the poor. Snyder argued that the congregation at Clifton should become a community that consistently and publicly embodied the biblical life they privately confessed. In the Bible, they encountered a Jesus whose life was given over to "the least of these." Now Snyder called them to be a community that witnessed to this truth in their daily lives.

Carolyn had been at home that Sunday morning caring for Christina, but Rob, Ed, and Murphy heard in Snyder's message a judgment on their rationalizing about opening a shelter. The next morning during breakfast, the four of them made the decision to begin a shelter at Clifton that fall. "We believed God was speaking through Mitch to our personal lives," Ed said, "and we hoped, to the life of the church. We would move ahead, and we would open the shelter. We would pay whatever price it took, physical or otherwise, to get it open by November 1."

With the city administration of Atlanta publicly scoffing at the idea that there was a large homeless population, the task of opening a shelter faced large financial and psychological barriers. Downtown Atlanta was in the initial stages of revitalization. New offices, hotels, and places to shop were being developed. Central Atlanta Progress, the major downtown business organization, had a special "Derelict Committee" to oversee problems with transients. Their main goal was to make sure that the homeless were "moved along" by the police and that the city was not hospitable in any way for homeless persons. There were, for example, no public bathrooms in the downtown area.

Quite aware of these facts, Murphy, Ed, Carolyn, and Rob went forward with their plans and spent the next two months making the necessary arrangements for the shelter at Clifton.

Materials such as cooking utensils and a washer and dryer were purchased. An agreement was worked out with the church, since some members of the congregation wanted it clear that the shelter was not the church's responsibility.

Carolyn and Rob moved into an apartment in Ed and Murphy's house at this time. The move was for practical reasons only, not with the idea that they would form a community. It just seemed to make good sense with Rob and Carolyn spending so much time at the church preparing for the opening of the shelter. The previous experiences both couples had with community kept them hesitant to try again.

On November 1, 1979, the night shelter at Clifton Presbyterian Church opened. Plastic sheeting protectively covered the carpet of the church sanctuary, and foam rubber mats donated by the Community for Creative Nonviolence provided beds for the homeless guests. Murphy humorously remembers the beginnings as inauspicious: "At the time Hannah [Murphy and Ed's daughter] was ten days old, Christina [Carolyn and Rob's daughter] was barely five months old, and Rob was flat on his back from back surgery. There was nothing wrong with Ed that we could see, so we decided to open up anyway." Given these circumstances, it was probably a blessing that initially the shelter was practically empty. On the first night, three people stayed there, and by the third night, there was only one. Street people were suspicious of Ed's efforts to get them to ride with him in an old van to Clifton. The shelter had opened during a time when a number of African-American children in Atlanta had disappeared and were later found murdered. People were fearful, and street people, as always, knew the best way to survive on the streets was to remain as invisible as possible.

Despite the initially low numbers, they kept the shelter open. They realized it would take some time to build up the trust necessary for people to come to the shelter. Murphy explained how their efforts began to reach people on the streets and the numbers increased:

> For the first several weeks, Ed and others just drove around in this old blue van we had, stopping and asking people if they wanted to come and spend the night in our church. You can imagine that most people thought we were crazy. But after that, word sort of got around that there was good food and a place to spend the night over at Clifton, and people started coming in. Soon, our problem was not to get people into the shelter, but to figure out how we were going to limit the number of people we let in. The church was so small, there just wasn't room to hold them all, and that was a very difficult thing for us.

With more people seeking shelter, the van was replaced with an old school bus and a pick up point was established near Grady Hospital in downtown Atlanta. Tickets were handed out for the limited number of beds available. It was often a chaotic, turbulent scene as people jostled for the available spaces. The attempt was made to choose the oldest, weakest, and sickest people in the crowd. It was a difficult task as up to a hundred people milled about, hoping for a place to spend the night.

The shelter at Clifton Presbyterian Church was the first free place of hospitality to open in an Atlanta church. An article about the shelter from *The Georgia Bulletin,* the newspaper for the Catholic Archdiocese of Atlanta noted with surprise that where the men sleep "is not any church-hall. This is the

HOSPITALITY WORK AT CLIFTON PRESBYTERIAN CHURCH, EARLY 1980S

CHURCH. Clifton Presbyterian Church has become the resting place—the sanctuary for the homeless."

Joining in the shelter work with Carolyn, Rob, Murphy and Ed were others from the congregation, among them was David Carr. David was a volunteer at the shelter the first night it opened. He had become involved with the church while finishing work on a degree from Carlton College, and Ed quickly invited him to join in the work of starting the shelter. David was very interested in deepening his commitment to a counter-cultural Christian faith and would soon join in discussions about forming a community. Additional volunteers followed, including Dick Rustay, who along with his wife Gladys, would later join the Open Door Community. After about three months of operation, a change took place among the guests at the shelter. Without being asked, they began to help the volunteers do the dishes, wipe off tables, and mop the floor. Stereotypes about the homeless broke down as volunteers from Clifton found that many of the shelter guests went to work every day at area labor pools. The volunteers also found themselves questioning their own values which judged people by how they looked or how much money they made.

Meanwhile Rob, Carolyn, Murphy, and Ed were coming to see that the shelter at Clifton was not enough. The need for shelter was vastly outstripped by the numbers of homeless persons now seeking it at Clifton and at the more traditional Union Mission and Salvation Army shelters. They began to urge other churches to offer hospitality to homeless people. Their message was that the offering of hospitality went to the center of Christian faith and practice. The Gospel they were committed to required direct face-to-face servanthood and community with the poor. It was not sufficient for Christians to give charity so that others could work with the poor in their place. Such surrogate charity maintained the barriers of wealth, class, and status between the giver of charity and the recipient. Through personal contact and building relationships with guests at the shelter, church members offering hospitality could come to see homeless persons not as charity cases, but as people to whom shelter and food were due in justice.

The advocacy of Rob, Carolyn, Murphy, and Ed for other churches to open shelters began to bear fruit when on January 14, 1981, Central Presbyterian Church, located across from Georgia's Capitol building in downtown Atlanta, opened a night shelter. Other churches rapidly followed. From its modest beginning at Clifton Presbyterian, the church shelter movement in Atlanta was spreading. As the winter of 1981-1982 approached, All Saints Episcopal, Oakhurst Baptist, and Trinity United Methodist opened shelters. By the fall of 1982, some sixteen churches opened their doors to shelter homeless people. The city government of Atlanta, however, had still not responded.

Despite their successes in urging other churches to open shelters, Murphy, Ed, Rob, and Carolyn were feeling that the pressures of running the shelter at Clifton heightened their own continuing questions about whether a congregational setting could adequately support an intense spirituality combined with social action with the poor. Did their hospitality work at the Clifton night shelter really build humanizing and liberating relationship between them and the homeless poor? Was this work promoting justice?

They were seeing that the justice they sought for the homeless, and for the prisoners with whom they continued to work, had to be more all-inclusive. It was a justice that went far beyond the prevalent sense of justice defined as the protection of individual rights in the pursuit of self-interest. Instead, it was a justice integrated with love and based on more biblical and even classical Christian traditions of the social nature of humans and the common good. This biblical and Christian understanding of justice urged that since all persons are members in the community, the justice of the community must be measured by its treatment of the most vulnerable. The possession of excess, when other people in the community do not have enough for basic necessities, is unjust. A society organized to protect individual rights and the acquisition of wealth, with no regard for the poor and no responsibilities toward the community as whole, was systemically unjust and must be rejected.

Murphy, Ed, Rob, and Carolyn were realizing the extent to which their view of justice was different from justice in American society. The execution of John Spenkelink in Florida in May of 1979 was a sign to them of the corruption of American justice. Ed had traveled to Tallahassee and participated in nonviolent civil disobedience at the time of the execution. They were seeing that a commitment to Christian work for justice required a fundamental change in moral outlook and way of life. American society regarded those who were poor and in prison with suspicion. Christian faith, however, must see them as human beings with needs we all share for respect, for love, for community. In an early interview with *The Georgia Bulletin,* Ed explained that they were trying to do this at the Clifton night shelter in terms of the biblical call to justice and new life:

> We take seriously the word "hospitality" and we are attempting to offer hospitality and not just shelter. Theologically, hospitality means to us trying to offer space where the men are not only sheltered and fed, but also are given friendship. And the basis for that is God's friendship with us.

Consistent with this view of justice in which persons are accepted and respected on the basis of their inherent dignity as persons created and redeemed by God, the shelter at Clifton imposed no rules of admission based on the criteria of "deserving" or "undeserving" poor. No identification was required, no questions asked, and a person could return as often as they wanted. Alcohol and other drugs were prohibited as their use could threaten the peace of the shelter. The shelter was to be a place where the homeless could be welcomed and feel at home. Still, as Ed pointed out in the same interview, they found it difficult not to make judgments about the homeless persons who came to the shelter: "Our middle class heritage has taught us to distrust the poor as people out to freeload. So we are in a constant faith struggle."

Carolyn, Rob, Murphy and Ed were finding that it was not easy for them to shake the competitive outlook of Americans that sees people as either useful or useless, and judges people by social indicators of wealth and status. They wanted to replace this outlook with a biblically based vision of human dignity and

CLIFTON SHELTER, EARLY 1980S

respect for all. Their theological and moral vision had been sharpened in the struggles within the congregation at Clifton. It had led them to their work with the shelter and continued in their advocacy for other churches to open shelters. Still as they considered their shelter work at Clifton and their advocacy, they still saw their own lives as too fragmented, and too far from true solidarity with the poor. They were finding it difficult to build much in the way of relationship between them and the homeless poor as they had hoped. They also hoped to start a soup kitchen were they could share meals with homeless persons. As they continued to study the Bible, now grounded in their work of hospitality, they started to talk about how biblical faith was always lived in community. They were joined in these discussions by David Carr. He now moved to an apartment near the church so that he could be part of these discussions and the move towards community.

As they talked together they also had before them the witness of past and present Christian communities. The Sojourners Community had long been influential in their thinking, and they also had contact with Catholic Worker houses, the Community for Creative Nonviolence, and in Georgia the Koinonia Community in Americus, Jubilee Partners in Comer, and a Cistercian monastery in nearby Conyers. Carolyn Johnson recalls that by the spring of 1980 they had come to a point in their work and discussions that, "if we didn't form a community all the talking and the theology would have been very hollow. If we wanted to keep the integrity of our discussions and who we were as Christians, then forming a community had to be our next step." Their conviction grew that membership in a congregation could not sufficiently support the kind of Christian life in solidarity with the poor and integrated with every sphere of life they thought necessary to be faithful to the Gospel. Additionally, they had reached the point where their beliefs were strong enough to overcome their fears from their previous failed experiences with community. On a Saturday in late May 1980, the four of them, along with David Carr, decided it was time to begin the work of forming a covenant community.

On June 28, 1980, they sat down together and started to write out what they intended their community to be. They scheduled a retreat for later that summer in Montreat, North Carolina, where Murphy's family had a house. There they put the finishing touches on their covenant to form a community. On July 24, 1980, they signed the covenant and the Open Door Community began. They "celebrated with prayer, communion and a party!" They covenanted "to share love and caring for one another, money, possessions, work, meals, parenting, worship, recreation and forgiveness." "As a servant community" they wrote, "we are empowered by the Holy Spirit to do Christ's work in the world. We are particularly called to a ministry of hospitality and visitation... Prison ministry, anti-death penalty advocacy, and night shelter ministry are the works we are called to do in Christ's name."

Ed had suggested the name of the community. It was based

on John 10:1-10 in which Jesus refers to himself as the open door by which the sheep enter the sheepfold. The homeless and the imprisoned needed doors opened for them, and in Christ the founders of the Open Door hoped that as a community they would do this.

Uncertainties faced all five signers of the covenant when they returned to Atlanta. For Murphy, Ed, Rob, and Carolyn the uncertainties were most directly related to questions about what affect their decision to form a covenant community would have on the Clifton congregation. They still harbored the hope that the Open Door Community could somehow be incorporated into the life of the congregation, perhaps as a different type of membership in the church. It quickly became evident that this would not be the case. As the news spread of the forming of the Open Door, most members of the church expressed feelings of trepidation and uncertainty. A few were genuinely excited about the possibilities it might offer the congregation. Others saw it as a threat to the unity of the church. They worried that it would lead Ed to neglect his role as pastor. Finally, some simply thought the whole venture crazy and unnecessary.

With this response from the church, Murphy, Ed, Rob, and Carolyn became increasingly unsure of their roles within the congregation and the possibilities for remaining within Clifton. In the congregation there had been some continuing aversion to the radical vision of the Gospel preached by Ed, and now that vision was embodied in a community associated with the church. Some resentment had also built up over the night shelter. Not everyone shared the enthusiasm of the Open Door Community members for this work and there was resistance to efforts to include the whole church in the shelter work. Additionally, Ed and Rob were feeling scattered as they tried to balance full-time jobs with the demands of the new community and the responsibilities of the night shelter.

For David, the struggle was not so much with the church,

but with his efforts to be both a fulltime student at Emory University's Candler School of Theology and a member of the community. This struggle was exacerbated by the living arrangements of the community at this point. While Rob and Carolyn lived in a basement apartment in Ed and Murphy's house, David was living in an apartment a few blocks away. The natural flow of life in the community and discussions about community life with Ed, Murphy, Rob and Carolyn living in close proximity while David was not around, led to his being excluded. David was sometimes late to community functions, or not able to make them at all. Despite everyone's best efforts, this situation was frustrating. David, too, felt the differences he had with the other community members, all of whom were all significantly older than him, married, with children, and established in their lives. As fall moved into winter, David faced a choice, either leave school or leave the community. Slowly and with great difficulty and pain he decided that he had to leave the community. He remained a volunteer with the night shelter and a member of Clifton.

As part of Ed and Murphy's discernment during this time, they (and baby Hannah) revisited the Catholic Worker in New York City. In September of 1980 they spent a week there learning more about the practice of hospitality in community. Though they did not meet Dorothy Day, Murphy recalls that while they were there she came downstairs to receive Eucharist. She died two months later. Murphy recalls that "I have always felt grateful for the experience of sharing that time of table companionship with her. I'm especially glad because I think that table companionship and the Eucharistic vision were the center for Dorothy."

In February of 1981, the four remaining community members decided to have a retreat at Our Lady of the Holy Spirit Abbey, a Cistercian monastery near Conyers, Georgia. At this retreat, they reached consensus that they should leave Clifton and find a place in Atlanta where they could live together, offer hospitality for the homeless, and continue the prison ministry. Ed would no longer pastor at Clifton and Rob would leave his job. They would all give themselves completely to the Open Door Community and its work. Ed summed up the motivation behind their decision: "We felt a new vocation emerge from our experience of serving God in the midst of the poor. We wanted to live with those we sheltered and we wanted to form an alternative style of Christian community—a residential community."

The covenant they had signed almost a year earlier proclaimed an integrity of life which they now believed could work only in an residential Christian community. This community would stand apart from the mainstream of American society and its values. They hoped that by living together in community they would be strengthened in their resistance to the dominant society and empowered for further solidarity with the poor. The decision to leave Clifton surprised few in the congregation; some were quite relieved. Clifton's own vitality, nurtured in the ministry of Ed, Murphy, Carolyn, and Rob, continued for many years after their departure. The congregation and other volunteers carried on with the night shelter work until the church closed in 2003. A non-profit group formed to continue the night shelter work, renting the space for a nominal fee from the Atlanta Presbytery. Looking back on their years at Clifton, in a letter to the congregation as the church was closing, Murphy and Ed wrote, "The Clifton days shaped the basic theology and sacramental practice of the Open Door Community."

© CHARLES HINKLE

CLOCKWISE, BEGINNING AT LOWER LEFT: MURPHY DAVIS, CHRISTIANA AND CAROLYN JOHNSON, ROB JOHNSON, EDUARD LORING, ROBERT BARRETT, NEELY AND SUSAN LORING, HANNAH LORING-DAVIS

4

ESTABLISHING COMMUNITY LIFE AND SERVICE TO THE POOR AT 910

THE DECISION BY ED, MURPHY, ROB, AND CAROLYN to leave Clifton meant that they had to find a place where they could live and work in community. They wanted to be in an area where homeless people would have easy access. The building needed to have enough space for a soup kitchen and plenty of rooms for community members and for the homeless folks they would invite to live with them. They soon learned that the old Women's Union Mission at 910 Ponce de Leon in the Ponce-Highlands area of midtown Atlanta was for sale.

When Ed and Murphy walked through the building with the

director of the Union Mission, they realized it was definitely big enough for the community and its work (some sixty rooms), though it was somewhat worn and old. The Ponce-Highlands neighborhood in which the building stood was in transition. There was a heady mix of small restaurants, bars, apartment buildings and cheap single room occupancy hotels, abandoned buildings and vacant lots, some small office buildings, and liquor stores. Just a mile or so from the heart of downtown and near several labor pools, it was an area frequented by homeless people, along with prostitutes and drug addicts. The Union Mission was pleased to hear that the Open Door planned to continue a ministry with the homeless, and were willing to sell it to the community for $150,000. To make the purchase, Murphy and Ed made a definitive break with mainstream life and sold their home. Contributions for the purchase also came from the Atlanta Presbytery and other donors. The resources from outside the Open Door would continue to be crucial as in the tradition of the Catholic Worker they refused government funding and relied on the generosity of congregations and other people.

On December 16, 1981 the Open Door Community moved into 910. Once there, they faced the massive task of making the place habitable. There was need for extensive scrubbing and painting before it could become a home and a place of hospitality. Murphy recalls: "It was a major excavation. We battled roaches and grime. When my parents arrived for a Christmas visit, I met them at the back door with a jug of Clorox and a mop. My greeting, 'Make yourself at home,' had never rolled off my tongue with such specific intent."

On Christmas Day, the Open Door Community initiated its work of hospitality in its new location with a dinner for one hundred homeless people prepared by two Atlanta gourmet chefs, Patrick Burke and Gary Kaupmann. On January 30, 1982, the community opened its doors for its first soup

© CHARLES HINKLE

FIRST MEAL, CHRISTMAS DAY, 1981

kitchen. Like the Catholic Worker houses of hospitality that preceded them, the Open Door saw the serving of soup as a central act of hospitality, and the homeless who come to eat are to be welcomed "as Christ." On this first day, 73 people were welcomed and served. Another intentional Christian community, Jubilee Partners, located in nearby Comer, Georgia, came and helped with the preparation and serving of the soup.

Don Mosely from Jubilee made enormous biscuits that were almost big enough to be a meal in themselves. Refugees from Cambodia living at Jubilee also lent their hands in service. They were stunned by the numbers of people who lined up for the meal. It was a day of contrasts. Refugees from Southeast Asia with first hand experience of U.S. military action and the warfare that continued even after the U.S. departure, ladled soup into bowls for U.S. citizens. Refugees from the "Third World" were helping to feed street people from the "First World." The refugees had never expected to see such poverty in the United States, which they considered the richest country of the world. By the end of February, the soup kitchen was regularly serving over a hundred people each day it was open. By May, the community had enough volunteers and the resources to keep the kitchen open seven days a week. It would eventually prove to be a schedule the community would have to adjust in order to remain faithful to its vision of hospitality and community life, as we shall see in chapter six.

In addition to the hospitality of serving meals, homeless people came to live with the Open Door Community as soon as it moved to 910. They pitched in to help with the work as they had at the Clifton night shelter. In the early days, when community members were still repairing and renovating the building, each person who came to stay at the Open Door cleaned the room he or she moved into. Robert Barrett had come with Rob, Carolyn, Murphy and Ed from Clifton, and soon Antonio Guillerme, Cuban born, was also invited to join them at 910. These were the first of the "houseguests."

As persons from the streets began to fill up the rooms, the new community started to work out some understandings of what they could expect from each other. With people coming from diverse economic backgrounds, from different races, and different creeds, there were plenty of opportunities for misunderstanding and conflict. Mistakes were made that sometimes led to intense conflicts. But there were also moments of grace when the community was surprised by love and life shared together. It was a daily struggle to create some level of order and an atmosphere of trust.

Ed tells the story of one young African-American man, Thony Lee Green, who was invited into the community shortly after it began. He was an especially enthusiastic worker and joined in with whatever task needed to be done. He mopped floors, carried in food donations, and helped with the soup kitchen. He often cared for Hannah and Christina, feeding them or changing their diapers. He became deeply involved with the life of the community and came to profess a deep faith in Christ. All of this happened within two months of his arrival at the Open Door.

But it was only about two months more before Thony was violently taken from the community. One day, right before the soup kitchen was to open, the end came for Thony's life at the Open Door. As the soup line formed, Georgia Bureau of Investigation agents appeared. They jumped the hedges around the front porches and burst into the house with pistols drawn. In moments they had Thony face down on the floor with a gun to his head. Over Carolyn Johnson's protests he was dragged from the house and driven off. No explanation was given and the officers refused to say where Thony was being taken.

After numerous phone calls the community learned that he was behind bars in the Fulton County Jail. Thony, they discovered, was a fugitive from St. John the Baptist Parish Jail in Louisiana. There he had been serving a sentence for an armed robbery at the Bucket of Blood Tavern. Convicted on five counts of armed robbery, he was to serve consecutive sentences leading to an incredible total of 480 years in prison! After his capture, Thony was sent to the Louisiana State Prison in Angola. Since that day, community members have at least once a year made the long drive to visit him. John Pickens, as a volunteer with the community, also sought legal recourse to reduce Thony's time in prison. Numerous appeals have failed, including one that made its way to the U.S. Supreme Court. The special relationship of the Open Door with Thony culminated in November 1995 when he was made a partner—a permanent member—of the community *in absentia.*

In addition to the work done by people from the streets who came to live in the house, the community also provided opportunities for an extensive number of volunteers from local churches, community organizations, and schools, and others to help prepare meals, serve soup, and aid in various tasks.

Coordinating these volunteers became a major work itself and has been handled by a variety of people in the community over the years.

Another type of participation in the life and work of the community formulated in this first year that has endured are "resident volunteers." These are people who commit themselves to live and work at the Open Door for six months or longer. As with the houseguests, a process began in these early days of the Open Door to establish the levels of trust and authority the community would share with these people called "resident volunteers." In chapter five we will discuss the evolving patterns of relationship within the community among permanent community members called partners, houseguests (now called "residents"), and resident volunteers.

In their first month at 910, the Open Door, like many other Catholic Worker or intentional Christian communities began a newspaper. Called *Hospitality,* Rob Johnson served as the newspaper's first editor. *Hospitality* regularly offers theological reflection on the life and work of the community. Over the years *Hospitality* has served as an important part of the community's voice in Atlanta and with supporters around the United States and in other countries. *Hospitality* has also provided careful analysis of justice issues connected with homeless persons and those in prison and on death row, coupled with a prophetic call for change on those issues, along with racism, war, sexism, and heterosexism. The first issue rolled off the presses in January 1982. It offered a brief self-description of the Open Door and explicitly drew connections between the situation of the homeless and prisoners and the community's work with them:

> As we opened our doors to share hospitality with friends who are walled out, we found it necessary to share that same hospitality with women and men who are walled inside the prisons and jails of our

state. God's good grace calls us to visit: a simple act of compassion where we meet again and again Jesus Christ, and learn of his suffering in a world filled with unforgiveness.

In the first years of *Hospitality,* advocacy for the opening of shelters in the city dominated lead articles. Though several churches had followed the example of Clifton Presbyterian and opened night shelters, the Open Door continued to urge more churches to open their doors to the homeless, and to press the city to open shelters. In February 1982 a group of people who had helped begin shelters started to gather regularly on Tuesday mornings at the Open Door. Out of their discussions regarding shelters and the needs of the homeless the more formal organization of the Atlanta Task Force for the Homeless eventually emerged.

During the first few years, as the community became more settled in their surroundings at 910, their relationships with homeless folks revealed two more pressing needs. In the summer of 1982 the Open Door started to offer showers and a change of clothes on a limited basis. The community was able to do this on a more regular basis when a shower room specifically for this purpose was completed in December 1983. Members of the community started to regard the offering of showers, like the soup kitchen, as a place where Christ is met under the guise of the homeless. Ed, writing in *Hospitality,* likened the showers to baptism, calling them "another Kingdom washing," and explained, "Washing, like eating, is related to the deepest mysteries of our sacramental communion with God in Christ. Showers and soup, shirts and sandwiches are offered and received here everyday. So is Jesus Christ."

In December 1982, the Open Door added breakfast to the soup kitchen meals it was offering to the homeless. Community members had begun spending periods of time on the streets to learn first-hand the needs of homeless folks, and to gain some sense of the experience of homelessness. During one such time on the streets, Ed and a resident volunteer, Mary Himburg, visited the city-operated Day Labor Service Center located downtown near Grady Hospital. The Center was started by the city in response to businesspeople who were concerned about the large number of poor people loitering downtown. Its purpose was to provide temporary employment and get them off the streets for at least the day. It did not seek to serve and empower those seeking work there, but rather to make them invisible.

As the Labor Center opened for another day, Ed and Mary met Alvin Dollar, its director. They discussed the dynamics of the labor pool. Ed asked, "What do these homeless people need more than anything else?" Dollar responded, "Breakfast." He told them of his pain in seeing people go off to a day of hard work on empty stomachs. Ed raised the possibility of the Open Door offering breakfast at the Center. Dollar's response was enthusiastic. By the middle of December 1982, the community had enough volunteers and resources to begin the breakfast. At first, the breakfast was served only one day a week. In January of 1983 another day was added. At this point, city officials sent down a directive stating that the Day Labor Center was a place for people to get jobs, not a place for people to eat. The breakfast would have to stop, they said, because it interfered with the efficient operation of the labor pool. Dollar reluctantly told the Open Door the news.

The community, however, was determined to continue serving the breakfast. They simply moved their serving line into the street in front of the Center. The street's name, Coca-Cola Place, witnessed to the paradoxes of corporate America and the city of Atlanta. The product now produced and sold worldwide had begun on the same block where the Labor Center currently stood. The immense wealth generated through

© CALVIN KIMBROUGH

BUTLER STREET CHURCH, 1996

the selling of Coke had benefited Atlanta in numerous ways through the philanthropy of the Candlers and Woodruffs who ran the company. The Coca-Cola Company itself, in becoming an international corporation, was increasingly intertwined with morally questionable business practices. Meanwhile, the city run by the political and business elite that had so benefited from philanthropy would not allow day laborers going off to minimum wage jobs to be fed by a volunteer group.

Alvin Dollar sought out the pastor of the Butler Street Christian Methodist Episcopal (C.M.E.) Church which stood around the corner from the Center. He asked Pastor Tom Brown if the breakfast could be served in the church basement. Pastor Brown invited Ed to worship and meet with the Butler Street congregation. Soon after, the church board also met with Ed, and then approved the serving of the breakfast in the church basement. Members of the church also volunteered to help with the serving.

The next Monday the breakfast was moved from the streets

to the church basement, and soon, three more mornings were added with the help of volunteers from the church. By the end of January, the breakfast was being served Monday through Friday. For this breakfast, the Open Door Community prepared the meal of grits, hardboiled eggs, fruit slices, multi-vitamins and coffee at 910. Loaded onto a van, the food was transported to Butler Street and served. Some two to three hundred people would line up outside the church and wait to come into the basement to sit and eat.

During these first years the Open Door also began to engage in actions that demonstrated its commitment to not only serve the poor with works of mercy but to serve also by demanding justice. On November 11, 1982, the community held its first "street action." This public protest was to dramatize the situation of the homeless in the city and call for the opening of shelters. A mock funeral was held at Woodruff Park in the heart of downtown Atlanta to raise public awareness of the homeless people who would die on the streets of Atlanta in the upcoming winter because of hunger, cold, and disease. Surrounded by the business towers, symbols of financial power, the community raised the question, "Why would people be left to die of exposure in a city with such wealth?" The community recalled that Atlanta had prided itself during the Civil Rights Movement as "the city too busy to hate." Now the Open Door Community wanted to know if Atlanta was "the city too busy to care." Local newspapers covered the protest which eventually left the park to march to City Hall where the community pressed its call to civic officials that shelters be opened.

The initial years at 910 also brought some change to the prison ministry. The community continued the practice Murphy had begun at Clifton Presbyterian Church of providing transportation once a month to Hardwick Prison for the families of prisoners. The hospitality offered on the trip expanded significantly when the Milledgeville Presbyterian Church began serving lunch for the families and drivers. The community also continued visiting and writing letters to prisoners on death row. As appeals ran their course and the state of Georgia began to execute people again, the community responded by participating in public actions of protest and civil disobedience against the death penalty.

During the Open Door Community's initial years at 910, some basic patterns of community life in solidarity with the poor began to emerge. The front yard of the Open Door Community became a place of gathering for homeless people. They gathered to enter for soup, for showers, for distribution of clothing and other basic necessities, and sometimes they gathered to catch a moment or two of sleep on the front steps of the house. Around the side of the house a public restroom was added to provide facilities scarce in the city of Atlanta.

Inside the house, on most days, there was constant activity. Monday through Friday, early morning cooks prepared the Butler Street breakfast, and then volunteers gathered to take the breakfast to the church and serve it. By mid-morning there would be community members and volunteers busy preparing for the day's soup kitchen or washing dishes returned from Butler Street. Trips up and down the steps at the back of the kitchen leading into the basement were necessary to retrieve food and other goods needed. (A dumbwaiter was not installed until the early 1990s.)

When the soup kitchen opened, the dining room's 36 chairs would fill rapidly. The serving of the meal, family style, usually meant it would be a few hours before everyone in the line at the door was served. Across the hall from the dining room, the living room would also be active as the soup kitchen proceeded. Furnished with some old couches and chairs, community members and folks from the streets would mingle, talking or reading newspapers. In a small office just off the living room a community member assigned to "phone and door" would hustle to keep up with calls and with the flow of homeless people coming from the soup kitchen to get a clean shirt, socks, a few toiletries, or to get their mail.

From time to time throughout the day, generous people would arrive, bringing donations of food or clothing, shoes or toiletries, blankets or winter coats. These had to be sorted and put away for later use. In the other rooms of the house, community members could be found working on any number of tasks: putting together the latest issue of *Hospitality,* organizing the next trip to Hardwick prison, or rounding up volunteers for next week's soup kitchen.

Down the hall from the living room and dining room, the shower room and clothes closet would be busy areas as showers were offered on certain weekday afternoons. Thirty or more people would line up to wash off the grime of the streets, and put on fresh clothes donated to the community.

Upstairs, Hannah, the daughter of Ed and Murphy, and Christina, the daughter of Carolyn and Rob, found space to play and grow. Child-care was a regular rotation as their parents and other community members made sure, as Ed wrote in *Hospitality,* to "serve Hannah and Christina with the same love and loyalty that Jesus gives us to serve the homeless and prisoners." A balance was sought in which parents and children would have enough time of their own together while also participating in the life and work of the community. It was often a difficult balance to achieve.

This brief description shows that the Open Door in its early years was typically a hectic place, and its activity required a disciplined form of communal organization. Times had to be scheduled for common prayer, renewal, and play. Decisions had to be made about what work would be done, who was going to do it, and when. Issues constantly arose as community members addressed the needs of those they sought to serve, and as they responded to the injustices inflicted upon homeless persons and those in prison and on death row. Further, within the community there was a group of people trying to live together with all their differences of temperament, education, culture, class, race, gender, and sexuality. As the community became rooted at 910, it began to discover the risks, the rewards, and the ongoing responsibilities of creating community that respected diversity and called each other to mutual accountability in a life of discipleship.

© CALVIN KIMBROUGH

CIRCLING FOR PRAYER AT 6:00 A.M. AFTER A NIGHT ON THE FRONT STEPS OF CITY HALL, FESTIVAL OF SHELTERS, 2005

5

LIVING IN THE BODY OF CHRIST: COMMUNITY LIFE, MEMBERSHIP, AND AUTHORITY

EARLY IN THE LIFE OF THE OPEN DOOR, the joining hands in a circle for announcements and prayer became a regular practice. This practice continues to the present. Ed sees the circle as "one of our sacred symbols. We picture it as a circle of disciples holding hands. As Murphy teaches us: the only chain we can stand is the chain of hand in hand." A circle forms before offering homeless persons breakfast, soup, or showers. Before community meals, a circle forms. Before leaving the house to provide transportation for family members to visit in prison, or for the community to participate in a vigil against an execution, a circle forms. Community members join together in a circle of prayer and shared discipleship.

The circle embodies the community's belief that reconciliation in Jesus Christ makes possible the Beloved Community in which persons live together in the full dignity of redeemed humanity. This belief was evident in the second issue of *Hospitality,* in August 1983. A front-page headline "Christ Himself Has Brought Us Peace" quoted from Ephesians 2:14, and Ed Loring and Carolyn Johnson wrote:

> God sent Jesus into the world that we might be reconciled to God and to each other. . . . Our bodies must be with the victims. . . . As we minister to the poor—as we share our food, our clothing, our money, our churches, our homes—we are transformed. In sharing, there is the transformation that makes reconciliation possible.

In continuity with this early statement of community purpose, Murphy drew upon Dorothy Day's emphasis upon the Mystical Body of Christ to write in a May 2004 *Hospitality* article:

> In the Mystical Body [of Christ] the "dividing wall of hostility" has already been broken down because of the courage of Jesus of Nazareth in confronting the power of death and oppression with life and hope. We receive the gift of unity and community because of this life of "hope in scorn of the consequences" (Clarence Jordan).

Through the dynamics of membership and authority, the community has sought to give structural expression to its commitment to form a circle of reconciliation. The commu-

© JOYCE HOLLYDAY

LEFT TO RIGHT: MURPHY DAVIS, HANNAH LORING-DAVIS, ROB AND CHRISTINA JOHNSON, CAROLYN JOHNSON, EDUARD LORING

nity desires to form one circle in Christ by braiding together different strands of membership and related expressions of authority. The structures of membership and authority are to create space and order in the community in which personal transformation may take place and hospitality may be offered.

When the Open Door began life at 910, the four founders became the first strand in the circle of membership and authority. The founders covenanted together to form the community. They committed to community life "for the long haul" and called themselves "partners." A second strand of membership and authority began when persons from the streets and prisons were invited into the community. They were called "houseguests." A third strand of membership and authority formed as people from more secure economic backgrounds joined the community for varying time periods. These community members were called "resident volunteers." A fourth strand of membership and authority formed as volunteers who did not live in the community came to share in the community's life and work.

In membership, the community addresses the mutual responsibilities and accountability needed for a life of shared discipleship. In the exercise of authority, the community orders its shared life, in both daily decision-making and setting long-range policy. In the exercise of authority, the community seeks first to order its life in such a way that inspires and empowers transformation of the members rather than deadens and dominates. Secondly, the community seeks to exercise authority so that order may be created and sustained for the offering of hospitality.

The community over the years has struggled to remain faithful to the call to be a community gathered in a circle as reconciled members of the Body of Christ. There has been experimentation, failure, and the need to start again. Murphy observes, "Sometimes we think that if we had known exactly what all of that [community life] was going to mean, we might not have started out on the journey. It is, after all, painful and hard to learn that we are not as good, as loving, as patient as our images of ourselves."

The basic patterns of authority in relation to the different types of membership began to emerge in the early 1980s as the partners and other community members confronted questions of authority in relation to a variety of issues. At one point, the issue was whether or not the expansion of federal government rules should lead the community to stop using government surplus cheese from the Food Bank. The partners saw continuing to get the cheese as entangling the community's hospitality in government regulations. The community's hospitality would be undermined by requirements to track how the cheese was distributed and the time and effort involved in observing the regulations. Some of the resident volunteers strongly disagreed. For them the government regulations were harmless.

With the community's hospitality at issue, Murphy saw this was "a time to reflect on how we make decisions, who is included in the decision-making process, and which principles of our common life and discipline are not simply up for a democratic vote." The community stopped using the cheese.

At another point, Murphy recalls, "we had a debate about whether somebody who had just showed up and really didn't like to wash pots could share equally in authority." Through such disputes the partners came to realize that there could not be a constant renegotiating of the community's basic commitments and way of life. Based upon their greater experience with and commitment to the life of the community, the partners would set the community's essential vision and practices and determine if a proposed change was consistent with that vision or not.

What emerged was a hierarchy of commitment, experience, and wisdom within the community. The partners, who were committed for "the long haul" and who had the most experience with community life would set the basic vision and practices of the community. Resident volunteers and houseguests would contribute in various ways to decision making, including regular meetings for consultation, and through daily interaction and discussions in shared life with the partners. Murphy explained:

> We had reached a point of realizing people bring a variety of agendas to the Open Door; and most of them leave after a while. So while we were not going to be mean and harsh, we needed to be realistic. The partners are the only ones committed to being here next year and beyond. Therefore there are some things we could not sit up all night debating.

This ordering of the four strands of membership and authority brought needed structure in the early 1980s. But it also remained a point of tension. By the mid-1980s, the partners faced difficult discussions regarding the community's direction. In April 1985, Carolyn decided to leave the community, and after about a year and a half of continuing with the community as a non-residential partner, Rob left. Though their decision was related to the community's work (which will be discussed in the next chapter), they also believed the leadership in the community was too rigid and did not allow enough sharing of authority.

Some of the houseguests also chafed under the structure of authority. At a house meeting in 1987, one houseguest objected to how decisions were made. "I don't know how you can have a real community when half the people here [the houseguests] have no decision-making position." At this point, partners or resident volunteers made the most basic decisions about the life of the community. Resident volunteers met with the partners once a week for a "weekly ministries meeting" where the daily operation of the community, such as work schedules for all members of the community, including houseguests, was set. Though houseguests were included in a monthly "house meeting" in which all of the community members participated, houseguests had little say in the setting of the daily schedule. Further, if a houseguest raised an issue that might cause a change in long term house policy, the issue was either deferred to the next meeting of the partners, or one of the partners explained why that policy existed and would not change.

Murphy responded to the houseguest's question by emphasizing that the house meeting was a decision-making body. Issues were brought up and decided upon at these meetings. But she also stressed that authority in the house differed according to level of commitment to the life of the community:

House policy is formed out of the common discipline

> embraced by the partners and resident volunteers in response to the call of Jesus Christ. Decision-making authority comes out of that shared commitment. Since houseguests do not share this commitment, they cannot fully share in the authority of the house.

Several houseguests agreed with Murphy's view. Since most houseguests were struggling with drug and/or alcohol addictions, they saw the need for a structure in which they could focus on those issues without taking on too much other responsibility. One stated: "The Open Door is a kind of sanctuary from the powers that beat us down, that put us on the streets and kept us there. I need rest more than I need responsibility right now."

Shortly after this house meeting, Ed reflected on the community's commitment to one circle around a common table and the need for ongoing conversion and conversation within the life of the community and its members in relation to authority:

> One of the ways I'm impressed with the power of evil is that after so many tries, and so many struggles, class structures still remain. I used to be embarrassed about the class distinctions between me and Jay [an African American houseguest who later became a partner in the community]. But as I see what is going on in this society, it is radical that Jay and I live in the same house, that Jay and I eat at the same table, that Jay and I worship the same God. That's about as good as you can discover in North American society today. That doesn't mean I'm giving up and settling for that—I pray, I work, I try to repent of privilege and class-mindedness in my own life. But I'm not thinking now, as I was five, six, or seven years ago, that we're going to pull off a kind of

> equality and mutuality inside this house that we can't do outside this house. The world is too much here.

Ed continued to emphasize the need for ongoing confession and conversion for the community to move toward being one circle of reconciliation:

> We have often confessed that the Open Door is not a place to come for those seeking a way out from the sins and demonic powers of modern America. For inside reside the same racism, sexism, classism, greed, desire for comfort, and hunger for short cuts that feed the evil and oppression outside. The difference at 910 is not in the presence or absence of sin and iniquity, but in our response to its presence and power in our lives. First comes confession. We are sorry: our hearts are broken. We repent. We commit our lives to being about the long, slow, error-prone process of undoing these sins. Secondly, we have a practice that encourages courage and frightens the Evil One. We often say to each other: "There is no such thing as a stupid question. Ask, ask, keep on asking."

By the fall of 1988 that "asking of questions" in relation to the exercise of authority in the community led to changes. The community participated in an "Undoing Racism" workshop, and also began to draw upon the wisdom of visitors from other communities. The label "houseguests" was changed to "community members from the streets or prisons." The new term still recognized a difference in how people entered the community and how their needs and responsibilities within the community might be different. But it also indicated that all who lived in the community were members.

At the same time partnership expanded. An initial development was to invite some who had come to the community as resident volunteers to become partners. The commitment to become a partner included the significant step of giving away all of one's possessions and investments. Elizabeth Dede who had first come to the Open Door as a resident volunteer in January 1986 after graduate studies in English, became a partner in April 1987. Gladys and Dick Rustay who came as resident volunteers in 1989, became partners in 1992. As we saw earlier, Dick had volunteered at the Clifton Church shelter. For several years after that Dick and Gladys volunteered with the community for various lengths of time when they could. In entering the community, Dick had left his work with Head Start, while Gladys left her work of teaching grade school. As with others who make the commitment to partnership they also gave up their home, all their savings, and insurance. They responded to Jesus' call to "sell all that you have and give the money to the poor and come follow me" (Mark 10:21).

The most significant change in partnership came 1989 when members from the streets or prisons were invited to become partners. Those who had lived in the community for two years or longer; who planned to be around for the foreseeable future; and who actively shared in the life, work and worship of the community could become a partner. Six "members from the streets and prisons" were invited to become partners: Jay Frazier, Ralph Dukes, Carl Barker, Willie Dee Wimberly, Willie London and Robert Barrett. In a festive service of worship the community welcomed and recognized their partnership in the Open Door. The leadership team became an administrative body within partnership. It no longer included all partners. Of the six new partners, only Jay Frazier stated interest in being on the leadership team and he was invited to join.

The other types of authority also saw some change at this time. In the fall of 1989, the entire community began to circle together on Monday afternoons (now Monday mornings) to decide on the week's work rotation and other issues of life together. This "house meeting" (now called "calendar check") replaced the "weekly ministries" meeting that previously had only included resident volunteers and partners. Community members from the streets and prisons now equally participated in setting the daily schedule of work and other activities in the community. Some community members from the streets and prisons who had belonged to the community for a year or more also began to exercise leadership within the community in taking the responsibility of doing house duty. House duty leadership involves a myriad of responsibilities and is essentially the person who coordinates all of the hospitality of the house while on duty. This will be discussed further in chapter six.

Those community members from the streets and prisons who did house duty also came to fully participate in the weekly meeting for house duty persons. This meeting addresses concerns specific to the responsibilities of being on house duty. Again, decisions are made here within the parameters of the community's long-term commitments. The decisions reached in both the house meetings and the house duty meetings are shared with the leadership team at their weekly meeting.

All of these changes had a noticeable effect on the activity of both the new partners and the members from the streets and prisons. The new partners came to more frequently exercise leadership in the organization of the work of the community, and to participate more fully in its life, worship, and political activism. Several members from the streets and prisons took on more responsibilities in the house and shared in leadership in such work as the breakfast or the soup or shower line.

The need to attend to the issues of membership and authority continued, however. After these changes, a community member for the streets observed, "I still see divisions here. They're divisions of class. A new resident volunteer has more

© CALVIN KIMBROUGH

© ROB JOHNSON

RALPH DUKES IN 1982 (AT RIGHT, ABOVE) AND 1992

say than a guy from the streets who's lived here for over a year." Nevertheless, he indicated a sense of membership that did not seem possible before these changes:

> There can't be equality. People are different. At least here when you're different, you're still valued. You're still treated like a person. The virtue of this place is that it shows we can live together—black and white, poor and privileged—if we respect each other and give each other a chance. It isn't perfect. No place is. But it's better than any other place I've been.

Ralph Dukes, who became a partner but did not want to become part of the leadership team, indicated his strong sense of membership due to these changes: "I would have died on the streets if not for this place. Being called a partner now might just be a change in words. But to me it means I've survived and I'm living, and this is home for me."

From the perspective of partners who did not come from the streets or prisons, these changes meant a new way of envisioning the circle of life in the community. Elizabeth Dede wrote:

> I had lived and worked with Jay, Carl, Willie, Willie Dee, Ralph and Robert for three years, yet I hadn't recognized fully their partnership with me; I hadn't seen completely how they were my family. Acknowledging their partnership publicly was my first step towards sight, and now I know that I had been blinded by the things that make me different from these new partners: my education, the color of my skin, my comfortable existence, and the privilege to choose to come to the Open Door. But with the eyes of faith, given to us by our brother Jesus, we can see Jesus in everyone, and so recognize our partnership together.

From the late 1980s through the 1990s this structure of membership and authority remained essentially stable. However, at the turn of the century the community faced challenges that led it to once again assess its structure. Among those challenges was the familiar but always difficult issue of creating community in the midst of race and class differences. Most of the partners and resident volunteers were white and middle class, while most of the members from the streets were black. Given the different levels of authority tied into membership, plenty of opportunities for misunderstanding and conflict related to race and class differences remained.

Within community life, a resident volunteer who is white

might say or do something that reflects an unconscious racism. If a black person from the streets confronts a resident volunteer about a racist comment or action, there is always the potential for an angry denial by the white resident volunteer who did not think of themselves as racist. Likewise, if a white partner calls a black member of the community to account for his or her actions, there is sometimes an accusation of racism leveled against the partner by the black community member. To build and maintain the trust necessary for talking through these issues remains difficult within the community.

In addition to race and class, a further complicating factor is that most of the persons in the community from the streets or prisons struggle with addiction. The discipline and structure needed to confront addiction and maintain sobriety inevitably leads to conflict and questions about trust. When those maintaining the structure are primarily white and middle class, while those struggling to overcome addiction are primarily black and from the streets, the difficult dynamics of race and class are intensified. There is plenty of room for misunderstanding, for manipulation, and for mistakes.

In the late 1990s and into the early 2000s several partners from the streets who had been with the community for many years left the community under difficult circumstances sometimes related to these issues.

Further, it was during this time that the community began to face its most difficult leadership challenge. In 1995, Murphy and the community confronted the hard news that she had cancer. Murphy was diagnosed with Burkitts' lymphoma, a form of non-Hodgkins lymphoma said to be particular to boys and young men in the tropical and low-lying areas of East Africa. Major surgery to remove several large tumors followed by five months of mega-chemotherapy put the cancer into remission. But six years later, in 2001, she was found to have a new primary tumor. Again there was surgery, followed this time by

85 days in the hospital for in-patient chemotherapy. Then in August of 2004, the cancer struck again, and complications of fungal pneumonia put Murphy near death. Murphy often turned to a passage from Isaiah 43:16, "Do not be afraid. . . . Your troubles will not overwhelm you. When you pass through fire, you will not be burned."

When Murphy was sick, Ed focused on being with her. The Open Door had to sustain community life in the absence of its founders and their charismatic leadership. Additionally, in April of 2000, Elizabeth Dede became a non-resident partner, moving from 910 to join the staff of the Prison and Jail Project in Americus, Georgia. She continued to participate on a regular basis in the community's Sunday worship and retreats at Dayspring and her column on the work of the Project became a regular feature of *Hospitality*. But her leaving around the same time as the partners from the streets were leaving, along with Murphy's cancer, contributed to the community's struggles around authority and leadership.

In response to these struggles, in the early 2000s the community intensified its emphasis upon continuing transformation of each community member. Murphy saw the challenge everyone in the community shares:

> The road to destruction sure is wide and easy, and always the most likely choice. But whether our struggle is to stay clean and sober or, more generally, to live a life of maturity and integrity, the practice must be exercised every day; the cross has to picked up every day. . . . This demands ongoing personal transformation, and it must be expected of each one if a community is to be truly alive.

The renewed emphasis upon the ongoing personal transformation of each community member took several forms.

For the partners, it was reflected in diversifying types of accountability. Ed and Murphy, as founding partners, are the most "public face" of the community, and within the community they are recognized as charismatic leaders having a moral vision and wisdom central to the life of the community. But they work within the partnership structure of the community, and all of the partners have responsibility for leading the community in worship, in setting long-term policies and practices for the community, and managing finances.

The partners who are part of the "leadership team" meet once a week to discuss issues facing the community, both immediate and long-term. Decisions are made by consensus and then shared with the rest of the community with response to the decisions invited. In addition to accountability to the leadership team, each of the partners also has a "pastoral friend" from within the community to discuss their life in the community. Additionally, an Advisory Board drawn from a variety of communities and churches provides important feedback to the partners. A fourth form of accountability comes from the fact that some partners, such as Ed and Murphy, are also ministers. Those that are ministers have accountability within the structures of their respective churches.

A final type of accountability for the partners is that the community as a whole emphasizes that the partners' most important expression of leadership is in their consistent commitment to live the disciplines of community life. Partners are expected to share fully in the life of the community along with the residents and the resident volunteers. Together, these members set the primary identity of the community, and on a daily basis hold each other accountable to these shared expectations.

For example, all members in the community are to participate in the faith life of the community, including Sunday Eucharist and times of daily prayer. All members commit to living simply. All who live in the community participate in the regular rotations of work and prayer (though in work assignments there has been recognition to some extent of differences in talents and physical abilities), and the community provides for each member's needs out of donations received. Community members do not have income beyond a small weekly stipend that is the same for every community member, whether partners, resident volunteers, or residents. In these practices, those living in the community form one circle of membership. This is also the case in terms of the shared vision of life (which will be discussed in more detail in chapter eight).

For those who come to the community from the streets and prisons, the community's commitment to ongoing transformation in shared life—the joining of hands in a circle—is first reflected in how new members from the streets and prisons learn the vision and practices of the community through a "pastoral friend." The partners did not develop (and have not developed) a detailed "rule book" handed out with laws to be followed. Instead, a "pastoral friend" is assigned to the new resident to guide that person in the life and practices of the community.

A recent (2005) Open Door document on "Structure, Discipline and Accountability" describes this weekly meeting. The pastoral friend and community member, "work with issues of orientation, maintaining sobriety, spiritual growth and development, interpretation of the community political context, leadership development, and the general issues of getting along in a diverse community." New members learn that they can live in the community as long as they want, if they accept the rules and responsibilities of life in the community. Positively, that life means strong support for a person's efforts to be renewed in human dignity that has been stripped away by life in the streets or in prison. The harsh struggle to survive in the streets or in prison is replaced by a community which provides love, a sharing of faith and worship, a secure place to live, and meaningful work.

Transformation through living in the community also demands difficult changes for those who come from the streets and prisons. There is always the issue of race. Ira Terrell who came to the community in 1991 said for him the biggest adjustment "was living with white folks. I just wasn't used to living with white folks." Since he had experienced so much racism over the years, including economic exploitation and physical abuse, he found it hard to now trust whites in the community.

Additionally, most coming from the streets or prisons are wrestling with issues of addiction, and staying clean and sober are requirements for shared life together. As part of the discipline to address addiction, members of the community from the streets or prisons generally do not have access to keys for the house doors for the first year of their living in the community. For these members of the community, the Open Door may appear as somewhat less than open. It is hard to live within the disciplines of the house, and also hard to see resident volunteers new to the community having more "freedom" with access to keys and cars than someone who has been in the community for six months or more. It can feel humiliating, and additionally so when the person in the community from the streets and prisons is older and black, and the new resident volunteer is younger and white.

Members from the streets and prisons who stick with the community for more than a few months begin to see the wisdom of the structure. Anthony Eunice gives this advice to those, who like himself, come from the streets to live in the community:

> First, learn to be still—physically, mentally, spiritually. Secondly, let go of expectations. Have an open mind. Create a desire to learn and to be open to the many

> different aspects of life here. We as residents have the responsibility of recovery and we have the responsibility of learning the community, and doing both of those on a daily basis.

Tony Sinkfield is a novice (a one-year period of discernment before becoming a partner) who also came to the community from the streets. He offers this advice:

> The people with the most experience generally dictate what's going to happen; which they should. The people with the most at stake here should be the ones who make the decisions. The Open Door was here before I came to live here and will be here after me. There's a reason why you don't get keys and make decisions right away. You see first hand how it doesn't work.

Resident volunteers, who join the circle of shared life in the community, are also assigned a pastoral friend who meets with them once a week and guides them in the life of the community. As with community members from the streets and prisons, there is no detailed rule book for new resident volunteers. However, the Open Door has developed some "Signposts" that apply to all members of the community, and a "job description" to give resident volunteers some sense of what is expected of them. These include commitments to live simply, to be aware of the power imbalances in the community, to not develop romantic relationships with homeless people, to dress appropriately. Resident volunteers typically live with the community and share in its work and faith for periods of three to six months or longer.

Although most of the resident volunteers are white, middle-class and college educated, there has been some diversity in terms of race, class, and education. Resident volunteers have been drawn from a variety of age groups, though those in their twenties, or older "second career" persons, often predominate. Those who apply to be resident volunteers are asked to provide a statement explaining why they want to come to the community and share in its life and work. Before coming as a resident volunteer, most have participated at some level with some aspect of the community's work. But those occasional experiences are different from actually living in the community. Resident volunteers frequently face challenges as their comforts and worldviews clash with experiences in the community and its work, along with the commitments of the Open Door.

Novice Lauren Cogswell reflected on those challenges:

> When I came here I wanted to make decisions, but I had no idea what it means to live with someone who is recovering from addiction and someone who has been homeless. Particularly as resident volunteers, we're used to having lots of privilege and lots of authority because that's our experience. We come from privileged leadership backgrounds, but we don't know what its like to live here. The folks who are here for the long haul need to make the decisions that shape the long haul life of the community. It is so important to have the folks who are bearing the consequences of decisions over the long haul and who have experienced the larger vision to be making the decisions.

The advice current and former resident volunteers offer to new resident volunteers, echoes advice residents from the streets offer to new residents. Chuck Harris advises a new resident volunteer to "try to understand the authority and structure, to learn the history why things are set up the way things are set up. People sometimes want to change a bunch of stuff and you need to understand why things are set up the way they are." Jodi

Garbison believes a new resident volunteer needs to come with "a real open heart and a willing spirit." Eric Garbison underlines the need for "commitments to sustain yourself, such as prayer. Come in with disciplines and be faithful to them." Lauren Cogswell sees that "coming here takes a lot of letting go. Be prepared to let go and have your life centered here."

For those who volunteer in the community's work but do not live in the community, there are also expectations and accountability. The community is clear in its vision and mission, and volunteers are quickly introduced to both. Before serving the breakfast or doing the soup kitchen, a there is a short meditation on a biblical text that sets the work to be done within the Open Door's vision of faith and hospitality. After the serving, time is set aside for reflection among those who have served, and those living in the community use this time to share the vision. Additionally, in the giving of service itself, community members instruct volunteers on how to practice hospitality, on what is appropriate and what is not appropriate in relation to each other and to the people being served.

Despite the sharing of the vision and practices that draw together the different strands of membership, significant differences remain between the different types of membership. Those who do not live in the community may at times have important roles such as house duty. House duty, as will be discussed more fully in the next chapter, is an important leadership role in which the person essentially runs the house for a certain amount of time during the day or evening. But volunteers do not shape the vision of the Open Door and they do not participate in long-term decision making within the community. Occasionally volunteers have been asked to stop coming because they engaged in actions deemed contrary to the community's vision and practice. Volunteers are expected to live within the expectations of that vision.

The community recognizes that those who come to the

community through the "back door" drive or are driven to the Open Door, while those who come to the community through the "front door" arrive by foot or bus and are seeking services. Both bring needs, but they are of different kinds. All who come are in need of transformation.

In addition to refocusing on the need for ongoing personal transformation, the community also moved to strengthen ties with other communities engaged in life and work similar to the Open Door. The community had always reached out to other communities for mutual support and accountability. In the community's earliest days, strong links were forged with Jubilee Partners and Koinonia. In March of 1985, the Open Door became part of the "Community of Communities" which included a variety of mostly Protestant intentional communities around the United States. Regular visits by leadership from those communities to the Open Door provided important guidance in the move to expand partnership. But by the early 1990s the Community of Communities folded.

In the late 1990s, the community turned toward a more ongoing connection with other Catholic Worker Houses. A close relationship especially developed with the L.A. Catholic Worker. There have been exchanges of resident volunteers and the leadership of the community travels each year to join in a retreat with other Catholic Workers. This three-day retreat provides opportunity for Bible study, prayer, worship, and discussions of community life. This has provided an important resource for developing community life. Gladys Rustay explained that these visitations "between our communities [were] to give strength and encouragement."

An additional development was that in August 2004 Nelia and Calvin Kimbrough joined the Open Door. As students at Emory University's Candler School of Theology they had known Murphy and Ed since the early 1970s. At that time they had discussed starting a community, though they eventually joined together with others to form the Patchwork Central Community in Evansville, Indiana. Changes in that community and their own desires to enter into the life of the Open Door brought them to the Open Door nearly 30 years later. Their years of experience in community life bring additional wisdom to the leadership team as they have now become partners.

Reflecting the struggles to live within one circle of reconciliation in the midst of differences in membership, authority, race, class, and the struggles with addiction, Murphy in the April 2004 *Hospitality*, observed:

> When our illusions die, we can learn that in a very real sense, authentic community is really not "built" at all. It has little or nothing to do with our magnanimous hearts, our long-suffering nature, or the astounding depth of our commitment. Deep authentic community has to do with offering our limited selves to God and praying for the wisdom and willingness to let God's Spirit form us for life together.

The willingness to let God's spirit form their life together working with the limitations of each community member allows the graciousness of God to be experienced in community life.

In the midst of the struggles related to membership and authority, the community continues to circle in prayer, seeking to be a circle of reconciliation in Christ. And because the circle continues, the difficult commitment to life together circled around Christ has borne fruit in community stories of both trust built and life shared. The circle of reconciliation, the joining of hands in Christ across differences of race, class, gender, and sexual orientation is powerfully transformative for those who stay long enough to let God work within them through the community. As Elizabeth's response to the new vision and practice of partnership indicated, changes in the structure of the community opened possibilities for her to see how she was joined with members of the community from the streets and prisons. Dick Rustay has seen how the daily work of the community is transformative.

> First, we are here to serve the poor. This work forces us to depend more and more on God's strength since we realize we only achieve a small fraction of what needs to be done. We learn to live with failure and understand that God's grace covers us, not for what we do or don't do, but for who we are. Second, we discover that living in community forces us to look at ourselves and realize change must be made in our own lives. Our sinfulness cannot be hid since life is no longer compartmentalized. Work, worship and play are all integrated, and it is impossible to hide your lifestyle and attitude from others. So change from within must take place. This change is painful, yet community love supports it.

Transformation, too, has been evident in those who have come to the community from the streets. Ralph Dukes first met Ed and Murphy when he came to sleep at the Clifton night shelter. Ralph had grown up in nearby Decatur and taught welding at Decatur High for several years. But as he has put it, "love of the bottle" led him to lose one job after another and he ended up on the streets. After the Open Door moved to 910 Ponce de Leon, Ralph frequented the soup kitchen, but his constant drinking seemed an insurmountable barrier to his ever living in the community. While Ed, Murphy, Rob, and Carolyn were out of town, Mary Himburg, a resident volunteer new to the community, invited him into the house. Those who knew Ralph's history expected that he would last a few days before he would resume drinking and thus be asked to leave.

Ralph has now persisted through over twenty years at the

© CALVIN KIMBROUGH

IRA TERRELL, 1992

Open Door. For many years he made the coffee each morning, rising early to prepare enough not only for the house but also for the Butler Street breakfast. As a member of the community, Ralph continues to join in the prayer and the varied work of the community, and in his spare time he reads novels and shares his love of blues music with community members and visitors.

Ira Terrell came to the Open Door in 1991. He had been on the streets for about two and a half years after spending nearly thirty years in Atlanta working a variety of manual labor jobs. Ira first started coming to the "grits line," the breakfast the community served at Butler Street C.M.E. church near Grady Hospital. After several months, C. M. Sherman who had become a partner after first coming to the Open Door from the streets, invited Ira to spend one night in the house. Ira remembers, "That bed felt so good. In the morning when I got up,

C.M. asked, 'Are you ready to go?' I said, 'Go where?' I've been here ever since."

Ira not only addressed his alcohol addiction, he also gave up cigarettes and became a long distance runner. He competes in the Peachtree Race and many other local events. Within the community, Ira has run the clothes closet and showers for many years, and also rises early to make coffee for the breakfast. At Sunday worship, Ira holds the cup for communion. "I really like doing that," he says, "When I get up and stand with that cup I look at the people and it gives me a good feeling. I tell them this is the blood of Jesus poured out for you and they tell me thank you. When I can't do that I just don't feel right."

In the 1980s Tony Sinkfield lived in the neighborhood around the Open Door. Then his crack addiction took hold and his life began to spiral out of control. Before long he was on the streets. In 1997 he came to live at the Open Door, but he stayed only until his first day off and then didn't come back. In the following years he tried various treatment programs, but none worked. By the fall of 2003 he was ready to come back to the Open Door. "I came here," Tony says, "to live differently." The community supported Tony as he entered St. Jude's, a drug addiction rehab center. He has gradually taken on leadership in the community, in particular helping to coordinate the Hardwick prison trip in which the Open Door offers transportation for family members of prisoners to visit their loved ones at the state prison in Milledgeville. He has also become a regular in doing house duty, along with being the person who orders the food and supplies. Importantly, he additionally provides leadership in various forms of the community's activism, including the Martin Luther King, Jr., Campaign for Economic Justice which began in the fall of 2005.

Stories such as that of Elizabeth, Dick, Ralph, Ira, and Tony reveal that trust shared in the circle of life in the community opens the possibility for mutually transforming relationship. But trust shared always involves risk. The differences in race, class, gender, and sexual orientation create ample opportunities for misunderstanding. And at times persons have sought to take advantage of and abuse the trust extended. The struggle with addiction has often led to persons leaving under regretful circumstances. On the one hand, for those who come from the streets and prisons, the Open Door attempts to become a home where wounds inflicted by the streets and prisons can be healed and persons can be restored to their full human dignity. After years of surviving based on mistrust and hustling, this process requires continuous effort by all involved.

On the other hand, for those who come to the community from positions of power and privilege—who enter from the back door, there is also the need for healing and conversion from individualism, fear, desires for control, self-righteousness and superiority. Deep faith in the redemptive power of love known in Christ, willingness to learn from each other, to hear correction of faults, and to have a sense of humor are some of the ingredients the community has found necessary to build the circle of reconciliation among people from different backgrounds and experiences. Joining the circle requires God's gracious love and a willingness to be receptive to the transforming power of God's love.

Murphy sees "many people articulate wanting community . . . but when it comes down to it, we learn that we have to be willing to do the tedious work of building community, striving for it, praying for it, sweating for it, hoping for it." Community life, she continues, has a transformational goal, "the larger purpose of helping us to grow in Christian discipleship: to grow in love and maturity." This love and maturity joins people together in the circle of community, Murphy writes, where we "practice the discipline of mutual care, to bear the pain and grief of love, and to nurture the courage to take action. In the community of faith and disciplined solidarity with the poor, we learn and re-learn that while nobody can do everything, everybody can do something. We all have a part to play in building the Beloved Community."

6

THE WORK OF HOSPITALITY WITH HOMELESS PERSONS

THE STRUCTURE OF MEMBERSHIP AND AUTHORITY as a circle of reconciliation within the Open Door not only provides a context for personal transformation, it also provides an order in which the work of the community can take place. Offering hospitality to homeless persons is the Open Door's most visible and ongoing work as a community. Community members are engaged in hospitality on a daily basis. In this work, community members respond to the suffering of homeless persons, and in doing so experience the injustices of American society, and their own limitations and failings, as they also experience the graciousness of God.

Community members in their hospitality offer words of welcome, meals, showers, clothes, a bathroom, a place to use the phone and to receive mail. A central text for the Open Door, as with many other communities that practice Christian hospitality, is Matthew 25:31–46. Christ is welcomed in the welcoming of "the least of these" which include those in prison and hungry and thirsty strangers.

The community's "Christ-centered" hospitality to the homeless revolves around the offering of meals. The community sees the Eucharist or Lord's Supper in which Christ is sacramentally present as the foundation for its hospitality. Ed writes, "At the Open Door Community we center our lives and engage our theological and political reflections on and around our meals. How do you eat? What do you eat? With whom do you eat? Where do you eat? These are the basic questions of discipleship life in America today. The answers reveal our truth. Our center is the Eucharist."

In the Eucharist, the crucifixion of Jesus is remembered and persons are united with Jesus in his life-giving resistance to the powers of sin and death. God's redemptive overturning of Jesus' execution by those powers—the resurrection—is renewed in the lives of those who share in his body and blood—in his life. The Open Door, in providing a refuge from the demeaning, dignity-denying crucifixion of homeless people, confronts the powers of sin and death. The community extends hospitality in response to God's hospitality to humanity in the self-giving love of Jesus' life, death, and resurrection. Reflecting Paul's words on God's hospitality (Romans 15:7), the community affirms that as God welcomes us in Christ, so we are to welcome others.

The loving quality of this redemptive Christ-centered hospitality is evident to homeless persons who experience the

Open Door as a place where they are welcomed as persons and treated with love and respect. The powers of sin and death are overcome as those rejected by society are welcomed with love. Names are shared as those serving wear name tags, and those who come in are offered a name tag as well. Pictures with the names of those who enter from the front door and those who enter from the back door are displayed in the hallways. Danny, a homeless man who came to live in the community, says of the Open Door:

> It is different because of the personal attention, the individual attention that they give you. Most other places you're just in line, you go through and you get your food and nobody talks to you. Nobody asks you how you're doing. Nobody asks how your day was. Here you get a lot of personal attention; a lot of handshakes, a lot of hugs, a lot of love. It is a Godly way of doing things.

To practice this Christ-centered redemptive hospitality, community members must open their hearts to those whom they welcome. In meeting Christ in homeless persons, community members experience renewed life and joy, along with a heartache that reflects the cross.

The redemptive life and joy come in the relationships that develop as basic human needs are met for food, for a shower and freshly laundered clothes, and, most importantly, for the simple recognition of another human being as worthy of respect and welcome. The life and joy come in meeting Christ in the homeless person. The life and joy come in the incredible patience, kindness, and humor extended by the homeless to those who live at the Open Door. As hospitality is extended in welcoming homeless persons, they in turn begin to share their life and their gifts with community members and other volunteers.

Sometimes this redemptive sharing of life even comes when one least expects it, or even desires it. Diana George, a resident volunteer in 2003–2004, tells a story of surprising joy one morning when she was in her room, "trying hard to concentrate, trying hard to block out the noise of conversations and soup kitchen pots and sirens and truck traffic," and then she heard singing. "Suddenly, the noise of the pots and traffic and people milling about the yard had arranged itself into music—beautiful, rhythmic, a cappella voices—in close Motown harmony, rich in the soul and gospel tradition of Black churches and side streets. Four men had circled in the drive and were making startlingly beautiful music. It went on for over an hour."

Sometimes the redemptive sharing of life becomes evident when you walk through the streets of Atlanta with long-time members of the community. One homeless person after another offers greetings, or inquires after the well being of community members, or discusses faith and politics, or gives thanks for a meal, a shirt, or some other act of kindness.

Murphy recalls the life and joy persons from the streets brought her as she has struggled with cancer. The diagnosis of cancer came quickly after many months of doctors trying to figure out what was causing her strange array of symptoms. The last of those symptoms was a "belly ache from hell" which immediately led to surgery. While she was in recovery, the word began to spread on the streets about Murphy's illness. The news was grim. The first prognosis was she had maybe 6 to 18 months to live. She was told that when she left the hospital she should go home, put her affairs in order and prepare for death. She recalls,

> By the time I finally came home, people in the yard were crowding around saying "we're praying for you Murphy." The first card I got in the hospital was one that one of our homeless friends brought and passed

around the front yard and was signed by about twenty people. Before other people even knew, they're passing around cards to be signed.

The joyful bond became even deeper when persons on the streets learned that Murphy would continue to receive care through Grady Hospital, the large public hospital that serves the poor in Atlanta. Many middle class persons greeted this news with unbelief and even anger. But, Murphy says, "Among homeless people there was a recognition of a new level of kinship. If you are going to Grady you must be with us. This was a kinship and camaraderie that was unasked for and was an absolute blessing."

If the joy comes in shared life, so too the heartache comes when persons you know and love experience the cross of being beaten down by the daily insults and harassment of a society that hates the poor. The heartache comes when the political and economic elite design yet another round of laws and public policy to punish the homeless with imprisonment. The heartache comes when the power of drugs and alcohol destroys a person. The heartache comes in seeing the suffering of those on the streets who are mentally ill, cast off to fend for themselves in an uncaring society.

The heartache becomes achingly personal when community members themselves have to say "no" in response to a homeless person's request for help. Mary Himburg, a resident volunteer in 1982–1983 wrote, "For every ten times I am able to say 'yes' I have to say 'no.' 'No. I'm sorry. You can't get a shower and clothes. I already gave out all thirty tickets.' 'No. I'm sorry. You can't stay here. We don't have any empty beds.' Each 'no' hurts and causes as much sorrow as the joy of ten 'yeses.'"

Lauren Cogswell, a novice who entered the community in 2003, tells the story of David who needed socks one morning when the breakfast was being served at 910.

"Could you bring me a pair of socks?" David asked.

"You can come in and get a pair of socks," I replied.

"I can't come in," David answered. "I am waiting for someone to drive by to pick me up for a job and if I am not there I might miss him. Could you just bring me some socks?"

"No," I said. "If I bring you some socks, then everyone in the yard will ask me for socks, and chaos will break loose. But you can come in, and I can give you a pair of socks." Round again we went.

"No," he said. "The socks might cost me my day's wages."

Like Mary, Lauren describes the heartache every resident volunteer sooner or later experiences at the Open Door. One's commitment to serve the poor runs into the complexities of economic injustice and racism (including one's own complicity in both). And one runs into one's own limits and the necessity of limits in trying to meet the continuing needs of the poor; and one's heart begins to ache.

For community members from the streets, serving people they once lived with on the streets carries its own unique form of joy and heartache. Anthony Eunice finds, "The expectation of providing assistance, to share in the work of the house is good; it's very good. It is an expression of the life of Jesus Christ, caring for the fellow person, showing the love through action, earning and building relationship." But he says, "For those of us who are recovering addicts, seeing that condition of the people who come in through the door is very moving. It can depress you. Some days it is tough to view people in that condition. I've known a number of them and know what they are going through."

Long-term members of the community are not immune from the heartache. Ed Loring tells the story of a woman, Mary Anne Cardell, who came to the Open Door late one night in the 1980s when he was on house duty. She had knocked on the door and she asked for a piece of paper and something to write with; Ed gave those to her, and she was also given a bit to eat. While she ate she began scribbling on the paper. When she was done eating she asked about staying the night. Ed told her the Open Door's policy: "We can't let you in when you've been drinking." He told her to come back tomorrow. She replied, "God is not dead. He is asleep. And He is in a very deep sleep." The next morning Ed went for a walk through some of the vacant lots that used to be all around the Open Door. In one of the lots he came across Mary Anne Cardell. Ed continues:

> She was dead. And the writing she had done that night, in part, was her suicide note. She had taken her suicide note and pinned it across her chest. And she was lying there in the field under an old and ancient oak tree with a six-pack of beer and a big container of prescription medication flung around like a wrinkled quilt. . . . I spent some quiet time before I came back home and called the police. I shared solitude with her. I asked her to forgive me. She answers still.

This is the heartache of knowing that there is always going to be another "no" that will have to be said, and knowing, too, that this "no" might lead to some harm or even death. How do community members continue serving the poor, knowing that their efforts in the face of realities of homelessness may not even impede a decline toward death?

The heartache can sometimes be so powerful that it threatens to overwhelm not only individual members of the community, but the life of the community itself. The sustaining of life and joy in the work of hospitality needs nurture. Nurture comes from the shared life in community, the prayer and worship—especially the Eucharist, and the shared reflection of the community in which the presence of Christ in the poor is affirmed. Nurture comes from the experiences of building redemptive relationships with people served. And nurture comes from taking the heartache and the anger it produces, and turning those into protest against the injustice that creates poverty and the injustices inflicted upon the poor; injustices that crucify Christ once more.

The community's recognition of the need to sustain life and joy in the work of hospitality has deepened over the years. At various points in the life of the community the heartache has threatened to overwhelm the community, and when this has happened the community has dug deeper into prayer and into life-sustaining relationships.

Murphy remembers December 1983 as one such time for the community. In that month, the state of Georgia carried out its first execution in nearly twenty years. John Eldon Smith was executed two weeks before Christmas. The community gathered with his family for burial at Jubilee Partners in Comer, Georgia. Then, during Christmas week, an intense cold spell sent temperatures plummeting, while shelters reduced their hours due to the Christmas holidays and lack of volunteers. The Open Door opened its dining room to take in people, and took hot coffee and soup out into the streets. Despite these efforts, by the end of the week more than 23 people had frozen to death in Atlanta. Murphy recalls:

> In the days and weeks that followed, I was heartsick and bone weary. I was disillusioned and angry. . . . I had been taught all my life that if I applied myself to a problem, I could solve it! We were well-educated people. We could change things. But what we were finding was that the longer we worked among the homeless, the more there were and the faster they were dying. The longer and harder we worked to abolish the death penalty, the more the American people clamored for executions. . . . I was losing my hold on hope as the pain and bitterness of loss threatened to engulf me.

Rob Johnson, writing in *Hospitality,* gave voice to the gloom that fell upon the Open Door in November, 1985. Simply maintaining what they had established in the four years since the beginning of the Open Door seemed to be draining away the community's life: "Our community is coming out of a difficult year—growing smaller. Overworked, re-evaluating our identity and structure, we have tried to slow down." He openly wondered about the future of the Open Door and its ability to continue with its work. Still he concluded, "We can only listen to God's call in our own lives and have integrity in our response."

Within the Open Door at this time there was a scarcity of resident volunteers to help with the work, and one of the original partners in the community, Carolyn Johnson, had decided to leave. She found work with Habitat for Humanity. Carolyn's departure in April 1985 made several difficult issues for the community more explicit, some of those having to do with membership and authority we discussed in the previous chapter. But another issue was the intense daily work of hospitality with the homeless, and the heartache of never having done enough.

Specifically, Carolyn and other community members believed that an emphasis on downward mobility and a life of solidarity with the poor had almost led to the exclusion of joy from the life of the Open Door. How was Christ present in the homeless poor who were sometimes drunk, drugged, disgusting? What did it mean to affirm this presence of Christ amidst the daily realities of soup lines and prisons? Carolyn recalled:

> I knew something was wrong when I would be at Bible study or listening to sermons and I'd feel like I knew what the next line was going to be. There didn't seem to be anything fresh; and there didn't seem to be any comfort. We didn't have any time for creativity, or for

the parts in ourselves that weren't tied so deeply to the work that we were doing.

When Carolyn left, her husband Rob still continued to work with the community. But about a year and a half later in early 1987, he left to work with the Atlanta Community Food Bank. His reasons echoed Carolyn's:

> For years I pushed myself in the things I wrote for *Hospitality,* and the ways I talked with people, to see life as a constantly downward pilgrimage. The cross and the crucifixion became central to the theology and lifestyle of the Open Door. They became too central, too emphasized. The balancing of a life of joy, and to experience in certain ways abundance, was difficult.

The sense that community life was being drained by too much emphasis upon the community's work and its identification with the cross did not disappear when Carolyn and Rob left. The struggle and tensions they identified had to be addressed. At the time of their departure the community was serving the breakfast at Butler Street five days a week. Seven days a week the community offered a soup kitchen. Showers and a change of clothes were offered three times a week. All of this was in addition to the daily work of answering requests for socks, a T-shirt or cap or work gloves, or maybe some aspirin, or mail, or to use the phone. The community was also committed to prison ministry and work against the death penalty. And too, the community was involved in street activism, urging the city to provide public toilets, to stop harassing homeless people, to build housing for the poor, and standing in vigil whenever an execution was scheduled. How could all of this hospitality work be continued and community members continue to be nourished in their spiritual lives so that they could face the heartache and celebrate the joys? It couldn't. Change was needed.

The departure of Rob and Carolyn helped push the community to begin revisiting its work of hospitality. Was the community trying to do too much? Could hospitality be sustained if the numbers of people served became too large? What was the relationship between hospitality and political advocacy? As with the changes with membership and authority, the community's nourishing of life in relation to hospitality evolved slowly and in response to further study, prayer, and discussion emerging from the community's experience.

The community took an important step in recognizing and responding to the need for rest and renewal in 1987. Although the community had retreats from the beginning of its existence, it lacked a place of its own for retreats, days off, and short vacations. Retreat houses were often too far away and were becoming increasingly expensive. A friend of Ed's from college, Bill Neely, came to visit at the Open Door. Ed shared with him the community's need for a place to rest. Bill's response was generous, "You find it; I'll buy it." After searching for a suitable place, the community found a few acres of land with two buildings (a farmhouse and a barn) near Ellijay, Georgia, about two hours north of Atlanta. The purchase was made in November, 1987.

Following a suggestion Murphy made, the place was named "Dayspring." The name came from Dorothy Day and from a verse in the Advent hymn, "O Come O Come Emmanuel," which said, "O Come blest Dayspring come and cheer our spirits by your advent here; disperse the gloomy clouds of night, and death's dark shadows put to flight." When Dayspring was acquired, the need for a place in which gloomy clouds of night and the shadows of death could be put to flight was most evident. In 1987, in the midst of the usual work of hospitality, there were five executions in Georgia, and in July of that year

© MURPHY DAVIS

DAYSPRING, 1989

Ed and Murphy's daughter Hannah had been in a serious tractor accident. The heartache of the life was deeply felt.

Community members quickly began to turn Dayspring into a second home. Murphy wrote, "our hopes for 'the farm' are realized: having access to the piece of earth outside the city teaches us new life rhythms and renews us for the demands of life at 910 Ponce de Leon." The importance of Dayspring as a place of rest and renewal has only increased over the years. Ed says simply, "I wouldn't be here without it." Gladys describes its importance for her. "It is amazing sometimes how renewing it can be. The connection with the earth is very healing." Dick notes that he and Gladys, "go faithfully to Dayspring on our days off. Just being away, just being there, in the silence, working the garden and the compost, is life-giving." For Tony Sinkfield, who came to the community from the streets, the time away is "refreshing" because "it is quite a bit different from being around here." Lauren Cogswell, as a resident volunteer, observes:

> Our lives here are really intense. Just living in community is intense. There are needs that everyone has,

> and there are the issues of coming off of the streets and addictions, and the needs of the house, clothes to be sorted, the bathroom to be cleaned, and the needs of the streets, desperate needs. Dayspring gives me a break from that intensity. When I walk outside the door at Dayspring no one will ask me for something. The solitude and the quiet and the green space are important to me.

Another important step for the community's nourishment in its work of hospitality came through its deepening connections with Catholic Worker communities. We saw in the previous chapter how the community reached out to other communities in the 1980s and 1990s for wisdom and support as it struggled with questions of authority and membership. In doing this, the Open Door began to develop important relationships with Catholic Worker communities and their tradition of hospitality and resistance. These relationships provided an important sense of solidarity with others in the difficult struggles of a life given to hospitality. And in this sharing of life, further nurturance of joy was made possible. Friendships developed, visits to each other's communities began to take place, and shared prayer bonded people in their concerns and celebrations.

In 1983, there was an initial reconnecting with the Catholic Worker when Open Door Community members went to the 50th-anniversary celebration of the Catholic Worker movement. There they met people like Brendan and Willa Walsh from the Viva House Catholic Worker in Baltimore. When the Open Door celebrated its 10th anniversary in 1991, Catherine Morris and Jeff Dietrich from the L.A. Catholic Worker came for the festivities.

The relationship deepened further in November 1997 when Open Door Community members joined with about 400

Catholic Workers in Las Vegas to celebrate the 100th birthday of Dorothy Day. Murphy was deeply moved by being invited to give the keynote address, calling it "one of the great honors of my life." As she spoke about Dorothy Day, she stated, "I look back over the last twenty years and realize that no one person, living or dead, has had a more profound effect on my life, my work, my belief." Murphy saw in the Catholic Workers kindred spirits who were "talking about the same things we were and looking for the same gospel resources for how to live a faithful life." Ed saw in the Catholic Workers people committed to prophetic action, people who are radicals, not liberals.

Out of this meeting came even closer ties with Catholic Worker communities, including exchanges in which members from the L.A. Catholic Worker and Open Door Community members would go to the other community and share in its life and work. For Gladys, this deepening of relationship with the Catholic Worker helps "with the unanswerable questions we face in working with homeless people and addicts, the disappointment." Dick finds the faith-grounded bringing together of serving and social justice as an important connection. "The more I learn about the Catholic Worker, the more I see the tradition of things we do here fitting with the Catholic Worker." The deepening connections with the Catholic Worker movement gave the community both a sense of being in a shared struggle and more faith resources for cultivating joy in the work of hospitality and community life.

As the community reached out for support in its community life and work of hospitality, it also made important physical changes to improve its ability to serve the homeless. Responding to the need for public toilets in the city of Atlanta, the community installed a public bathroom in the basement area of the house in 1986. This bathroom replaced portable toilets the community had placed in the backyard. In order to provide a more hospitable space and to provide for a cleaner food preparation and dish-washing area, the community's dining room and kitchen were renovated in 1997 and reopened in early 1998. Additionally, through 1995–1997 a large section of the basement, which had been crawl space, was excavated and finished off to provide more space for food storage, food preparation, and laundry facilities.

Another development in the community's hospitality was the addition in 1995 of the Thursday evening Harriet Tubman Medical Clinic to the already existing Soul Care Foot Clinic. The Foot Clinic had begun in June 1983 when Ann Connor, a Registered Nurse, began to care for the feet of homeless people. She bathed and soaked the people's feet, and anointed them with salve. She also listened to each person, hearing of their aches and pains and when needed referred them for medical treatment. The Foot Clinic expanded when Heather Bichol and Joanna Whatley from the Georgia Baptist Nursing School joined in the work of the foot clinic as a senior project that they continued after graduation. They put together a training manual and recruited others to wash and care for the feet of the homeless.

Volunteer doctors and medical students from Emory University School of Medicine began the free medical clinic. Dr. Briggetta Jann was the first doctor to lead the clinic, but when she returned home to Switzerland in the fall of 1997, the clinic temporarily ended. However, before she left she created a prescription fund in honor of her son Roald Rees who had died. A few months later, Marisa Rogers, a fourth year medical student along with Dr. Pierre Felix, and Dr. Pam Logan, revived the clinic. Over the years a number of physicians and medical students have come once a week to see twenty or so people, offer minor treatments, write prescriptions, and when necessary refer those they saw for further treatment at Grady Hospital, Atlanta's large public hospital that offers medical care for the poor.

© CALVIN KIMBROUGH

SOUL CARE FOOT CLINIC, 2006

The need for spiritual nourishment intensified when Murphy faced cancer in 1995, and again in 2001 and 2004. At these times, she and the community were joined in prayer by a vast extended support network of people. The community found itself receiving hospitality, as Murphy did when her first card came to her from the homeless people in the yard. One aspect of this hospitality came in the form of bone marrow drives. Lauren Cogswell organized these drives as Murphy's doctors believed a bone marrow transplant would hold the most hope for Murphy after the recurrence of the cancer in 2004. By the spring of 2005, hundreds of people had signed up for the national bone marrow registry as over 16 different gatherings were held for this purpose. Churches, civic organizations, and seminaries were among the groups that sponsored bone marrow drives.

In the early 2000s, several significant changes came to the community's offering of hospitality. Murphy's illness, coupled with the aging of the core leadership, and a decline in numbers of resident volunteers, led the community to begin trimming back some of its services. Though it was painful to make these changes, in doing this the community was seeking a better balance between hospitality, political activism and time for prayer and reflection.

A move in this direction first emerged through a change the community initially did not welcome. Since December 1982, the community had served a breakfast in cooperation with Butler Street C.M.E. Church located near Grady Hospital in downtown Atlanta. When the leadership at Butler Street C.M.E. decided to use the church's basement for other church programs the serving of breakfast there came to an end. On September 25, 1998, the community served its last breakfast at Butler Street and reluctantly moved the breakfast to 910. But in time the community came to see this move as helpful for its practice of hospitality. The serving of the breakfast came to be more deeply grounded in times of prayer and reflection, both before and after serving; something that could not be done in the limited time available when serving at Butler Street. By beginning with prayer and reflection and ending in the same way, both community members and volunteers were provided a regular opportunity to share the joys and heartaches of their serving within a prayerful context. It was a time to do theology rooted in the works of mercy and committed to the works of justice.

This deepening of the connection between the work of hospitality and prayer and reflection had long been something the community sought to do. Back in 1990, Dick and Gladys had raised the issue of the need for more Bible study and reflection in the community. Ed agreed on the need to use existing times for prayer "to center around the themes of scripture and reflection upon common life, and that we need more political reflection and encouragement to activism." Attempts were made to do this at various times, but with the moving of the breakfast from Butler Street to 910, the community moved to regularly integrate times for prayer and reflection prior to and following each time of serving the poor. It continues to be a practice before and after each breakfast and soup kitchen. Murphy explains what the community does and why:

> It's a process built into our life together, called by liberation theologians the action-reflection method. We begin with reflection on scripture and prayer; we work together; we reflect. We hope to build a praxis of liberation: our thinking, our action, and our worship are clarified and deepened as we consciously bring them into interaction. Reflection informs action; action makes reflection concrete. It all becomes an expression of worship. We hope that all of this will help us to move toward mature faith and integrity. Often, it all seems very ordinary. Some days, we are moved beyond words by the depth and power.

In a circle of chairs or around a table, those who serve the meal reflect upon the work of hospitality in relation to biblical faith. They come to connect the slaughter of the innocents by Herod with the slaughter of the innocents through poverty, homelessness, imprisonment, the death penalty, and war. Or they connect the fleshpots of Egypt that tempted the Israelites after the Exodus with addictions, consumerism, racism, sexism. Or they link Jesus resisting the temple system to resisting today's linking of religion and empire.

Persons also share their own struggles with how their lives are being transformed by serving homeless persons. Volunteers, students, businesspeople, teachers, residents of the community from the streets, resident volunteers, partners, and usually a currently homeless person or two who helped serve the meal, sit together and reflect on the way the Bible illuminates hospitality with homeless persons. It is a challenging and often life-changing seminar in the way God graciously acts to liberate human beings, to free persons for new life, particularly through God's presence with the poor.

Other changes to better integrate hospitality with community life came in January of 2000. At this point the community decided to serve the breakfast four mornings a week and the

PHOTOGRAPHS © CALVIN KIMBROUGH

BREAKFAST CIRCLE, 6:00 A.M., 2005

soup kitchen four days a week. At the same time, the showers were moved to the morning creating space in the afternoons for calm and rest. By 2005 the community was serving the breakfast twice a week, the soup kitchen twice a week, showers twice a week, and essentially "closes the house" from sundown Friday to 5:00 P.M. on Sunday when Eucharist marks the beginning of the new week. This schedule allows community members one day off per week, but also allows time for rest, for community meetings, for activism, and for community prayer and reflection. In this schedule there is the commitment to the long haul, to staying in place as a way to love the poor and to build trust with those who have been abandoned by the larger society. Ed reflects that "we do the amount of work we can sustain with joy, rest, and radical politics." In these changes, we can see how the community has adapted to changes within the community's membership and responded to the need for a rhythm of life in which hospitality can be sustained.

Perhaps two of the most important and ongoing forms of hospitality at the Open Door remain central in the midst of the changes, namely, "phone and door" and "house duty." Phone and door involves exactly what you would think, answering the phone and door. During the hours when the house is "open" the person on "phone and door" checks mail for homeless persons whose mail is sent to the Open Door, responds to arriving donors of food and clothing, or tracks down a community member who has been called. This person is often the first to offer a welcome to people who come to the Open Door. If the house is "closed" these responsibilities continue for the person on house duty, though during those times there are usually fewer people who come to the door.

In addition to these duties, the person on "house duty" welcomes people to the Open Door and has an important leadership role. This person coordinates all of the hospitality offered by the community. Mike Vosberg-Casey, a resident volunteer for several years, sees "the person who does house duty at any point in time as the decision maker for what's going to happen right then. Everybody who does house duty learns how to make decisions within the framework of decisions that guide the house."

House duty is done in shifts that run from 8:00 A.M.–4:00 P.M. and 4:00 P.M.–8:00 A.M. The house duty person works closely with the person on phone and door, and with all of the people who do the myriad of activities that make possible the breakfast, the shower line, and the soup kitchen. The house duty person does things that can be mundane (yard clean-up or emptying wastebaskets in the "public areas" of the house), directly hospitable (handing out sandwiches and blankets to homeless people at 7:00 P.M.), a form of specific leadership (leading prayer at the evening meal), or difficult (mediating a dispute among homeless guests in the front yard).

The person on house duty is most directly responsible for saying "yes" or "no" for the many requests for help that come

SOUP KITCHEN IN THE FRONT YARD AT 910, 2004

during the day or early evening. In the winter, the house duty person decides whether or not to open up the house for people to come in and sleep in the dining room to get out of the cold. To be on house duty is to be engaged in the work of hospitality for most of a day or night. It is, says Chuck Harris, a resident volunteer, to be engaged in "making a welcoming place." Eric Garbison, a resident volunteer, describes house duty as "shepherding" in which "an order is created in which hospitality can be offered." Lauren Cogswell echoes Eric, "House duty is shaping and overseeing the inner life of the community that enables us as a whole to offer hospitality." She relates this to welcoming people into the community's circle of life:

> We are always a community under formation. We always have new people coming into the community whether they be residents, or resident volunteers, or guests, who don't necessarily practice the life the way we practice it or don't understand the life. So there is always a need to have someone to provide solid leadership, be that at a meal or at prayer or at the door resolving a conflict in a creative and loving way.

In trying to meet needs, the house duty person often enters into conversations with persons from the streets that reveal the ways in which homelessness is connected with institutional injustice. Heather Bargeron, a former resident volunteer, tells the story of a homeless man who came to the Monday breakfast:

> He requested some MARTA tokens to get to the VA hospital. He was suffering from some kind of skin rash. He had tried for several months to treat it with topical ointments, but he got no relief. He had a few tests done at the VA and the doctors thought it was related to exposure to depleted uranium. He was a veteran of the first Gulf War in 1991.

Those on house duty hear stories of arrests for not having an I.D. that leads to prison time that leads to loss of work. There are stories of having to wait most of a day at Grady Hospital to get a prescription filled. There are stories of police harassment. There are stories of one personal disaster after another which slowly but inexorably draws a person into homelessness as relationships with work, friends, and family unravel.

The community brings together the heartache and joy of the work of hospitality with worship through two annual events, the Festival of Shelters and Holy Week on the Streets. The Holy Week on the Streets began in 1985 when the community became aware that March 31 was Palm Sunday and on that day, the last day of March, most of the night shelters for homeless people in the city of Atlanta would close. Murphy sees that during the Holy Week on the Streets, "We go out onto the streets during Holy Week to remember the Passion of Jesus Christ as we walk the via doloroso of the homeless poor." She recalled her first 24 hours on the streets during Holy Week in 1985:

> I thought I knew something about the streets. I though

> it wouldn't be that bad. It was supposed to be 50 degrees that night, certainly warm enough to be out. What I learned forever changed my feelings, thoughts, and sense of urgency about homelessness. The entire night was an experience of being moved on. A 50 degree night is not warm. Time became very heavy.

Elizabeth tells of a Columbia Seminary professor who spent 24 hours on the street during one Holy Week. He came to see that "homelessness is like a slow execution. The monotony of the day, the exhaustion, the punishment your body takes from the weather, the lack of healthy food, the slavery of labor pools—all lead to death. And we sentence so many of the citizens of Atlanta to this punishment."

Elizabeth also remembers the times that she and others have directly experienced how the police clear areas of homeless people. One night during Holy Week they attempted to sleep on the steps of the Fulton County Health Department across the street from Grady Hospital. It had been a place frequented by homeless people looking for a place to sleep. Around 12:30 A.M. they were awakened by an Atlanta police officer who yelled, "Get up! You can't sleep here. Lots of big people drive along this street, and they don't want to see you. You've got to get up and move on!"

For those who came to the community from the streets, such as Ira Terrell, Holy Week on the Streets is a time to share their knowledge of being homeless. "People look to me to give them some sense of what it is like to be on the streets." Anthony Eunice found that at first "I had a lot of hesitancy returning to the streets. But after coming back there was gratitude. Simply sharing my experience being homeless and addicted was helpful."

The Festival of Shelters began in 1989. The community decided to draw upon the Festival of Booths in the Jewish calendar, Sukkoth, held in the late fall to call attention to the coming of winter and the inevitable suffering cold weather brings to people on the streets. Ed explains the connection between the Festival of Shelters the community observes and the Festival of Booths:

> The Festival of Shelters is a liturgical event which calls us back to the right road so that we may move ahead into the house of justice and peace. The Festival of Shelters is a reenactment of the ancient path from slavery in Egypt-land toward the land filled with milk and honey. For 40 years the people of God wandered in the wilderness eating manna and living in shelters. Existence was precarious, and dependence upon Moses and God was clear and concrete. And then the people entered Canaan, living in their own houses and preparing their own food. Their lives began to be like our lives today—for those of us who sleep in our own beds and eat from our own kitchens. So God gave to homeowners a special observance—the Festival of Shelters—so that we would never forget the experience of homelessness and remember that the God of our good gifts is the same Yahweh who teaches us to see brothers and sisters in the homeless ones and join, today, in their journey toward housing and justice.

During the week-long Festival of Shelters community members keep vigil at Woodruff Park, and each day the community gathers there for worship. Dick Rustay explains:

> In preparation for the Festival of Shelters, we studied the eighth chapter of Deuteronomy, where the Israelites are constantly reminded to remember: to remember that God sustained them in the desert; God brought

© CALVIN KIMBROUGH

FESTIVAL OF SHELTERS, 1989

> them out of slavery; God is still the Provider and Sustainer even when there is now plenty and people live in houses. For some of us, who had never been homeless . . . the question was "How can we remember?" So we went into Woodruff Park and listened and looked.

Whether it is during the Holy Week on the Streets or the Festival of Shelters, in these times on the streets, the community reduces the distance between itself and the people to whom they offer hospitality. Community members both experience the harshness of homelessness and the hospitality the homeless offer. Sharing a "cathole" with a homeless person, or sitting down together to eat in a soup kitchen offered away from the Open Door, or sitting together in a park trying to get warm as the sun rises, community members taste something of homelessness. Those who regularly host homeless persons are hosted as they spend this time on the streets. Such experiences inevitably deepen one's compassion for homeless persons and sharpen one's sense of the injustice daily faced by those on the streets.

While on the streets with homeless persons, community members find a joy in the hospitality shared with them. At the same time the heartache nags as they experience the harsh realities of how life on the streets is a crucifixion. Both the Festival of Shelters and Holy Week bring those experiences to prayer and to a public call for justice. In this way both sum up and give prayerful expression to the redemptive hospitality the Open Door offers, a hospitality that is graciously transformative of the persons who offer and receive it, and a hospitality that seeks the transformation of a society that harshly judges and degrades the poor.

7

THE WORK OF HOSPITALITY WITH IMPRISONED PERSONS

THE OPEN DOOR'S HOSPITALITY FOR THOSE ON THE STREETS is intimately connected with its hospitality for those in prison. This close connection was dramatically illustrated back in the mid-1990s when Murphy was on the phone with Charlie Young, a man who had been on death row since 1976. As they talked she told him of "the other Charlie Young" who had been invited into the community from the streets a few days earlier. Charlie on the phone asked Murphy to describe "the other Charlie" at the Open Door. Before long he was excitedly shouting, "That's my father!" Murphy grabbed a book that had a picture of Charlie being interviewed on death row. She ran into the hall and found the other Charlie Young. Turning to the picture she asked him, "Do you know this young man?" Charlie began to jump up and down, joyfully yelling, "That's my son! That's my son!" Murphy took him to the phone, and father and son were reunited. The father had faced the slow execution of life on the streets and had lost track of his son; the son faced the more efficient execution by the state and had lost track of his father. But now they were united. Charlie stayed with the community until he was able to move into his own apartment. He remained a regular volunteer. His son eventually won a decision that stopped his execution and he was given a sentence of life.

An experience like those of the "two Charlies" makes the link between the homeless and the imprisoned even more poignant for the community. Ed sees the link between homelessness and imprisonment as related to the loss of the practice of hospitality in the church and society and the criminalization of the poor:

> Our nation's greatest evil is that as a people we now hate, fear, and despise the poor. As the Judeo-Christian ethical influence mixed with the development of Western culture, the poor were seen as 'ambassadors of God,' or opportunities to 'do good.' The stranger within the gates brought an opportunity of hospitality for which the homeowner was thankful. Today a stranger brings hostility, and the homeowner wants strangers jailed. Throughout most of our history a stranger represented the divine or a friend; today a poor person, unknown and hungry, represents evil and stands as an enemy.

Ed's analysis is supported by the experience of the homeless. Homeless people often spend time in jail for "crimes" related to their being homeless, like public urination or loitering. In Atlanta, "sweeps" of the city take place before major conventions. Homeless people are cleared from the streets by arresting them, and they are held in jail until the convention ends. Then, those arrested find their charges dismissed and they are released. But the arrest kept them out of sight during the convention.

At other times, arrests do not result in the dismissal of charges. But persons from the streets will plead guilty for "time served" just to get out of jail, whether they were guilty or not. The result is a growing list of convictions on a person's record, and convictions for such crimes make it even more unlikely that they will be hired for work, and so the cycle continues. The majority of people behind bars in Georgia and nationally are poor, disproportionately African American, and neglected and despised by the larger society. This is even more the case for those who are behind bars on death row.

In analyzing the connections between homelessness and prison, the Open Door sees the need for God's redemptive hospitality not only in response to the meanness of the streets, but also in response to the criminal justice system, with its jails, prisons, and state executions. The community's practice of hospitality reflects its conviction that in the resurrection God confirms Jesus' enactment of the reign of God, of liberation from sin in all its death-dealing forms. Members of the Open Door join with Jesus in the God-inspired struggle for liberation and life against sin and death by visiting those in prison, rejecting the institutionalized revenge of inordinately long prison sentences and executions, and advocating for redemptive justice in response to wrongdoing.

This redemptive justice affirms the dignity of each human being and refuses to regard those imprisoned as unworthy of love and as people for whom there is no hope. In the face of human brokenness, the Open Door seeks to bring healing and to affirm liberation and the life of reconciliation instead of enslavement and death. The Open Door seeks to enact Hebrews 13:3, "Remember those who are in prison, as though you were in prison with them; those who are being tortured, as though you yourselves were being tortured." Murphy observes that we can hardly remember those in prison as though we were in prison with them if we know nothing about prison and never visit prisoners.

Over the years of the Open Door's existence, Murphy has provided the primary leadership in the community for its work of hospitality with prisoners. Recall that while still at Clifton, even before the formation of the Open Door, she organized a major anti-death penalty demonstration in Atlanta and then founded the Georgia office of the Southern Prison Ministry. She has led the way in visiting death row and speaking out against capital punishment. Through her consistent visitation and advocacy Murphy has stood in solidarity with the imprisoned and those on death row. As Murphy faced death in her struggles with cancer, she became even more profoundly connected with those she visited on death row.

Murphy has drawn strength from her relationships with persons on death row. One such relationship was with Warren McClesky who was executed by the state of Georgia on September 25, 1991. Murphy had visited him on death row for thirteen years. She had gotten to know his family and with them and Warren had experienced the horrible tortures of the judicial process in which an execution date is set, a reprieve then granted, and another execution date is later set. McClesky's case had wound its way through the appeals process until it finally reached the U.S. Supreme Court in 1987.

At the heart of McClesky's appeal was a study by David Baldus which showed a clear racial bias in the application of the death penalty. The Court accepted Baldus' study as valid, and agreed that there was racial bias in the application of the death penalty. But the Court refused to deal with institutional racism. The Court concluded that "taken to its logical conclusion [this racism] throws into serious question the principles that underlie our entire justice system." When McClesky was executed, Justice Lewis Powell confessed that his vote to uphold the death penalty in *McClesky* was his greatest regret.

Murphy last saw Warren McClesky in the waiting room the night he was executed. He had asked forgiveness from the family of the person he was convicted of killing. Murphy saw in him a person who had "moved toward a peace and serenity" she had "never seen in another human being." She saw that, "The courts, the media, the prison officials, the threats, and even death itself lost power in Warren's life." Murphy saw in him a sense of peace that did not change as he left to be executed. This is what she drew upon as she faced her own deadly illness:

> For me, the really important resource through those times was the fact that I had sat with so many people facing their own death. I know people who on the day of their deaths, managed to maintain their dignity, their hopefulness, their love, their humanity, their capacity to not be eaten alive by fear. The people on death row taught me how to face death. These people who society says have nothing to offer—I can tell you what they have to offer. I'm living witness to what they have to offer. The hope, the love, the lack of fear I was able to experience, was a gift from many of those people.

Ed, in an article for *The Catholic Worker,* wrote of the identity he saw between Murphy and those on death row when the disease struck her for a second time. He and Murphy had been visiting Terry Mincey, their last visit before he was to be executed the next day. He was the first person in Georgia executed by lethal injection. Ed wondered if any of the medical personnel who would do the lethal injection got their training at Grady, the site of Murphy's treatments, or through Emory University or the Morehouse School of Medicine, both of which use Grady as places for medical training. After they had visited Terry Mincey, Murphy grew ill and two days later was taken to Grady "where needles did a different kind of work." Ed wrote:

> While kneeling beside Murphy . . . I saw Terry. Murphy's bed became a gurney. We were holding him down. He jerked and cried. The doctor's needle slipped several times, then back again. The needle whirled and stuck deep into his flesh. Terry looked up at me. "Do something. Do something," he screamed. I tried to say something, but only a guttural grunt gurgled from my throat. I was afraid!

As Ed and Murphy's experiences show, in the hospitality of visitation, community members build powerful relationships with prisoners. But members of the Open Door not only visit those in prison, they also facilitate visits between prisoners and their family members.

Before the Open Door began, Murphy was organizing trips for family members to visit their loved ones in prison. What is known as "the Hardwick Trip" goes back to 1977. In Murphy's work to help organize a national demonstration in Atlanta against the death penalty she met several mothers of prisoners on death row. She learned of the need for family members to be transported to visit their loved ones in prison. Murphy drew upon the resources of the Southern Prison Ministry and started to organize transportation to the state prison at Reidsville some five hours from Atlanta, and also to the prisons near Milledgeville, about two hours from Atlanta. Relatives without

© CALVIN KIMBROUGH

ELIZABETH DEDE, RIGHT, ARRANGES A HARDWICK TRIP, 1998

reliable cars or no cars at all would rarely have been able to make either trip.

When the Open Door began, Carolyn Johnson joined with Murphy to help with driving another vehicle. Over time, others began to offer to drive people to the prisons for visits. In bringing family members to visit, Murphy said, "We began to experience the joy of restored relationships, especially as mothers and children were reunited."

In January 1982, Murphy received a phone call from Rev. John Campbell, the pastor of First Presbyterian Church in Milledgeville, Georgia. He said, "We've got a whole lot of prisons down here, and we've been thinking that maybe we ought to do something. And so I'm calling you." Murphy went in March to meet with church members and she described the transportation the Open Door had been providing to family members of prisoners. Church members asked how they could be helpful. Murphy described her response, "It seemed obvious enough as I thought, 'Well, what do we church folks do best:

Fix dinner and eat together!' So I said, 'How about lunch?'" Church members immediately agreed.

In September, 1982 the church doors opened, and the drivers and passengers for the prison visitation were invited in for food and hospitality. With the help of additional volunteers to drive, and Atlanta-area churches donating vans for the trip, as many as 100 family members each month are given the opportunity to visit their loved ones. Murphy describes the gathering at the church:

> The people fill the fellowship hall and circle the tables. We hold hands and introduce ourselves and share our lives and pray for our friends and family in prison. We give thanks for the gifts of food and welcome. And in those times we are one: we know God's presence among us in the breaking of the bread.

One of the grandmothers who went on the prison trip for many years stopped when her grandson was released. She wrote a card of thanks to the pastor at Milledgeville, saying, "This church is a do-body. Not a church to just *talk* about love, but one to *do* it." One mother wrote the Open Door: "The trip to Hardwick means a great deal to me, for it is a time of fellowship with our loved ones; a time to show them that through it all we care, we're concerned, and we love them." Murphy tells the story of Sonya, who participated with her children in the Hardwick trip:

> After a year of the family riding with us on the prison trip, Sonya's husband was released from prison. She wrote us a letter, telling of his homecoming, thanking us for the many rides, and sending a contribution from her tiny income for the continuation of our ministry. It seems like a small thing. Because of the willingness of

> churches to offer their vans and individuals their cars, because of the countless volunteers who give a day of their time once a month, because of the hospitality of the Milledgeville Presbyterian Church. . . . Because of all this, one family managed to stay together. The daddy got out of prison, and his children knew who he was and eagerly jumped up to cling on his neck. The wife and the husband had a monthly visit to share news and decisions, discuss their lives, and dream together. The end of a prison sentence for one family meant coming home instead of wandering into the midst of strangers.

Joanne Solomon, who for many years organized the trip, reflected on the signs of the Kingdom in the life-giving ties formed in this prison ministry. She wrote that when those on the Hardwick trip gathered in a circle to pray before lunch, God's liberating love was evident:

> As we joined hand to hand in a wide circle, I couldn't help but think of the bonds this circle represented: bonds not only between friends new and old, but within these families as well; sources of strength and encouragement in difficult circumstances. I thought of these families who would enter the prison buildings, allowed only the required picture identification, and no gifts for their loved ones but themselves. I was reminded of God's gift to people everywhere and in all circumstances of life. The gift of Jesus who gave freely of himself so that we might all know... healing and restoration to the broken places in our lives.

Rev. Bill Morgan, a former pastor of First Presbyterian in Milledgeville, echoed Joanne's view, "Our people are getting to know these aren't some terrible strange folks in prison. These people deserve respect, and we want them to feel part of our family." At the same time as the community tastes and shares the liberating presence of God in these visits, it also continues to give voice to the suffering and the death, the despair, and the destruction that prison brings.

PRISON PRIVATIZATION AND SLAVERY

While family members are visiting their loved ones, Murphy will sometimes lead a tour of the prison grounds. In this "Hardwick teaching trip" Murphy describes how after the Civil War the 13th amendment banned slavery except as punishment for crime. She tells how Southern Senators fought to include that phrase and in the South slavery was re-invented through the "convict lease system" which lasted until the late 19th century. It was replaced by "chain gangs" which also subject convicts to hard labor and abuse. Chain gangs were ended in Georgia in the 1940s, but hard labor has continued under different forms to the present. Corporations have turned to running prisons for profit, prisoners are employed at low or non-existent wages, and in some states the chain gang has reappeared.

Murphy urges that the ties between poverty, racism, and prison continue in what she calls "prison slavery." She tells the story of her first encounter with prison slavery when she visited the Georgia State Prison at Reidsville in the spring of 1978. When she drove onto the prison grounds "as far as one could see there were groups of men, mostly black, bent over, laboring in the fields. Here and there were uniformed men on horseback with rifles across their laps, overseeing the work." Murphy comments on the rise of corporate owned prisons, "However you want to dress it up, the traffic of captive human beings for the purpose of private profit is slavery." She speaks out against seeing prisons as "an industry" that can help the economic development of towns. "To build a future for our communities on the practice of human bondage is to collaborate in the design of disaster. To attempt to 'save' ourselves and our communities by creating jobs for growing number of overseers and keepers to hold neighbors in cages is to 'sow the seeds of injustice and reap the whirlwind.' "

Private companies making money from imprisoning people have little or no incentive to decrease the prison population or to engage in any sort of rehabilitation programs for the prisoners. A prisoner wrote in *Hospitality* of his experience with this system:

> Prison creates a mindset of institutionalized slavery. To avoid the drudgery of doing nothing, prisoners work. This work exposes the value of prisoners to the prison system and officials. As long as the prisoner does what he or she is told, the prisoner has value. If the prisoner doesn't work or do what he or she is told, then the prisoner is punished. Those prisoners that feed into the system of working hard and staying out of trouble are labeled as good resources, and as a consequence are compelled to serve longer prison sentences. Parole always seems to be just beyond the grasp of those that work the hardest and do the best in prison.

The Open Door, through *Hospitality* articles, letters, and leafleting campaigns, has continued to seek to illustrate the realities of the growing prison-industrial complex.

Another community member and partner who has become particularly focused on prison work is Elizabeth Dede. In 1999, Elizabeth participated in the Freedomwalk, organized by the Prison and Jail Project. The Prison and Jail Project was run by John Cole-Vodicka, who along with his wife Dee and their children, twice lived at the Open Door. In the 1980s, John had worked as a lay chaplain at a 2,300-cell county jail in Oakland, California. He and Dee then lived at the Anderson Hospitality House near the Federal Women's prison in Anderson, West Virginia, where they offered hospitality for family members visiting prisoners. From there they had become members of the Open Door Community. In 1993, John's commitment to activism on behalf of prisoners led him to found the Prison and Jail Project as a grass-roots civil rights organization devoted to protecting and working on behalf of prisoners and their families. The Project is based in a small office in Americus, Georgia, that it shares with the local NAACP chapter.

Elizabeth's participation in the Freedomwalk in 1999 connected her with African Americans in Smithville, Georgia, who were struggling against abuses perpetrated by the local police chief and judge. As the Freedomwalk prepared to go through Smithville, the small group of marchers was threatened with arrest if they continued. One of the women from Smithville, Carrie Thomas, said, "Chief, this is our town and our Freedomwalk, and you'll just have to arrest us." The arrests took place. A month or so later the trials were held. The judge, who had been so abusive, agreed that the ordinance that had been the basis for their arrest was not constitutional. The charges were dismissed.

Hoping to continue the spirit of the court challenge and victory, many of the African American women in Smithville, including Carrie Thomas, wanted to move forward with opening a community center. Elizabeth joined with the organizing, taking a six-month leave of absence from the Open Door to work with the Prison and Jail Project on helping get this community center started. Elizabeth found this work was calling her into a different relationship with the Open Door Community. With the agreement of the leadership team she became a "non-resident partner" in August 2000 when she moved to Americus, Georgia.

Elizabeth continues to be part of an ongoing monitoring of the city court, the police department, and city government in Smithville. Voter registration ultimately led to the 75 percent black majority ending white political domination in the city. With the change in city government, there has been change in the police department and court. As the police department became African American, police harassment ended, and there are now so few arrests that city court meets only once every three months instead of every month. Elizabeth also participates in an after school program in which local children are tutored and helped with homework.

An important part of Elizabeth's ongoing close relationship with the Open Door is her regular column in *Hospitality* that draws upon her work with the Prison and Jails Project. Elizabeth reports on the conditions of jails in Georgia and the injustices in the criminal justice system. Elizabeth's column helps to continuously remind readers of *Hospitality* that the injustices resulting from poverty and racism contribute to both homelessness and abuses within the criminal justice system.

THE DEATH PENALTY

The Open Door finds the dynamics of economic injustice and racism are most intensely active in the death penalty, and Georgia's use of the death penalty repeatedly shows these dynamics. In the 1972 Supreme Court case *Furman vs. Georgia,* the death penalty was held to be unconstitutional because it was applied in a manner that was arbitrary and capricious, and "pregnant with discrimination." Justice Potter Stewart wrote in the decision, "if any basis can be discerned for the selection of these few to be sentenced to die, it is the constitutionally impermissible basis of race." The "new and improved" death penalty statutes that emerged in response to this test of constitutionality were supposed to remove the bias of race in the application of the death penalty. The McClesky case discussed above and further research suggest otherwise.

Though about 29 percent of people in Georgia are African American, on death row nearly half are African American. Of the 113 people on death row in Georgia in January 2005, 54 are black, and 3 are Latino. The Death Penalty Information Center reports that through the end of 1990 the Chattahoochee Judicial District in Georgia (which includes the city of Columbus) had imposed the death sentence on 20 people, more than in any other district in the state, and nearly twice as many as Atlanta which has three times the population. More than half of the black men sentenced to death were tried by all-white juries after the District Attorney used his discretion through peremptory challenges to remove every black potential juror. The DA sought the death penalty in nearly 40 percent of the cases where the defendant was black and the victim white, in 32 percent of the cases where both defendant and victim were white, in just 6 percent of the cases where both defendant and victim were black and never where the defendant was white and the victim black.

The vast majority of the executions in the United States take place in the states of the old Confederacy. A recent count by the Death Penalty Information Center showed 781 of 948 nationwide executions took place in those states. The influence of race and poverty in the use of the death penalty in the United States continues to be well documented. The Open Door, in its work for the abolition of the death penalty, continually tells the stories that illustrate how executions reflect the dynamics of race and poverty. When John Eldon Smith was executed in December 1983, Murphy wrote:

> It seems that we as a people have spent literally millions of dollars to try, condemn, cage, and kill one human being. In the process, the careers of various politi-

> cians, lawyers, judges, law enforcement and prison officials have been enhanced. . . . And the attempt has been great to assure the public that something has been "done" about crime. The law works, you see.
>
> One more human being is dead in Georgia, the execution capital of the United States. Others will follow. They will be poor and they will be selected according to our patterns of racial discrimination. Beyond that "method" they will be a randomly selected few who will be offered up to pacify the public rage and frustration over the way things are.

In addition to the dynamics of race and poverty, the community also argues that political and religious leaders use the death penalty to distract people from attending to the root causes of violence in American society. Murphy observes that people find it is easier to focus on "bad people" and to execute them, rather than to creatively respond to the cultural idealizing of violence, along with the economic injustices that contribute to crime. She says that people feel that "if we'd just get rid of those bastards, we'd all be safer; we'd all be better off." Society seeks to blame persons for its shortcomings, and the easiest targets are the poor and racial minorities who have few resources by which to defend themselves and are already despised and feared by society.

Community members often point to the fact that public support for the death penalty waxes during economic hard times and wanes in times of economic prosperity. In 1935 at the height of the Depression, 199 people were executed in the United States. In 1944, 124 were executed. The numbers continued to decline as the economy improved so that in 1967 there were only two executions. With the rising and ongoing economic anxieties of the last twenty-five years the number of executions rose.

These economic and racial factors in the use of the death penalty are further fueled by a cultural conviction that violence and vengeance are the best responses to wrongdoing. Theologian Walter Wink has pointed to a deep cultural belief in "redemptive violence" in which violence "saves" a society from evildoers. Action heroes in Westerns, detective and crime movies regularly use violence to eliminate evildoers. Within the culture as a whole, there is a continual demonizing of the poor and racial minorities.

Within this cultural context, is it easier to kill those who are poor and/or members of racial minorities or other "unwanted" groups of people, and it is also easier to kill those considered beyond human and social concern. Those to be executed are portrayed as incapable of human feeling and are judged inhuman. Their heinous crimes both "prove" their inhumanity and demand "pay-back." No hope or even desire for their redemption or rehabilitation is expressed. Rather, "justice" demands that they be put to death so that society may be rid of them. This desire for vengeance was expressed with brutal bluntness by an editorial in a Georgia newspaper after an execution:

> It is with pleasure this week that we bid a hearty "good riddance" to Henry Willis III who was electrocuted at the Georgia Diagnostic Center near here last week. Willis, who killed Ray City police chief Ed Giddens as he pleaded for his life, lived on death row at taxpayer expense for far, far too long. Criminals like Henry Willis III, the others executed before him, and those currently under death sentence are human waste. Executing them should come as easily to a civilized society as flushing the toilet.

In a society where such convictions are stated publicly, by not only newspaper editors but also politicians, prosecutors, and even worse—preachers—the Open Door realizes that most people will find it hard to hear the Gospel message of love, of accountability for wrongdoing for the sake of redemption and reconciliation. Murphy observes:

> When the moral tone is set by political opportunists, the language of love and reconciliation sounds silly. It is always easier and more popular to have a quick fix and settle for revenge and fear. But this does not help us become more compassionate and helpful to the wounded ones.

The Open Door is most dismayed by the preachers and church members who urge the death penalty. For the Open Door, support of the death penalty is a sign of the appalling corruption of so much Christianity in the South and the United States. Christians should be able to see that the death penalty is wrong because it gives power to the state that belongs only to God and because it denies the possibility of conversion, of reconciliation, of new life. The death penalty perpetuates the very cycle of violence in the world that Jesus rejected in the Sermon on the Mount; rejected when a woman caught in adultery was brought to him for judgment (John 8:1–11); and rejected when he told one of his followers who had drawn a sword to violently defend him at his arrest, "Put your sword back into its place; for all who take the sword will perish by the sword" (Matthew 26:52). Murphy writes:

> Jesus always held out the possibility that any human can change. Turning away from sin is always a possibility, and it is not for human beings to say that the possibility no longer exists. Violence always produces grief and brokenness. Capital punishment produces more grief and brokenness. It does not help the victims who have

> already suffered grief and brokenness, nor does it lead anyone toward healing and restoration. It only heaps brokenness upon brokenness; grief upon grief; murder upon murder.

Members of the Open Door Community, in visiting and exchanging letters with prisoners on death row, have found that even persons who have committed the vilest of crimes, and who in justice belong behind bars, are still human, have wisdom to offer, and can share love and tenderness. Murphy often tells the story of Jerome Bowden, a mentally retarded African American who was executed by the state of Georgia. Before his death, Jerome offered his simple philosophy of human life. He said, "Peoples was not made to dog around, peoples was made to be respected."

Murphy and Ed also recall that when Hannah was still a baby, they brought her along on a visit to death row. The inmates carefully cradled her and cooed with the unabashed joy of proud relatives. Murphy observes:

> The media portrayals of bloodthirsty criminals devoid of humanity were obviously incorrect. The mystery of each person as a child of God, and the possibilities for their renewal through love, are not the realities presented by media stereotypes of those who are sent to death row.

The Open Door sees that its relationships with persons on death row are grounded in the Gospel call for love and solidarity with those most despised by society. Murphy writes:

> When we look to death row it pushes us to the outer limits of our compassion and our theology. Besides, it's hard enough in these days to defend, advocate, or

> stand up for any poor people. And when we get down to death row, we're generally talking about guilty, poor people. But still there are great resources to grapple with ethics around the death penalty. In every great faith tradition, we are admonished to compassion, to welcome the outsider and the stranger, to mercy. These are high ethical norms in most traditions. . . . But isn't it interesting that at the very heart of the Christian faith is an act of state execution? Isn't it amazing that the very sign and symbol for us that identifies us and our faith and our sanctuaries is a cross? An instrument of state execution. . . . But we're always trying to turn this story into something else. . . . But the cross was not so attractive to the people following Jesus when they saw him hung up on it in occupied Palestine: no more attractive than the electric chair or lethal injection is to us today. . . . What might have happened to church history, if we had consistently referred not to "Christ crucified," but to "Jesus the Jew executed by the state"?

In addition to visitation of those on death row and political resistance to the death penalty, the Open Door also resists the death penalty and its dehumanizing violence when it offers a funeral for a man executed by the state. The community has done this on several occasions. Joe Mulligan was executed by the state of Georgia in May 1987. Following his request, his relatives, friends, and members of the Open Door gathered with the Jubilee community at Jubilee's Koinonia House. From the hall the coffin was carried under the hot Georgia sun about a half mile along a dirt road to the cemetery. As persons grew tired, others in the funeral procession stepped forward to share in the pallbearers' task. Those who carried the casket saw their drops of sweat fall upon it like tears and these were joined by those who wept more visibly.

© CALVIN KIMBROUGH

BURIAL OF JOE MULLIGAN, JUBILEE COMMUNITY, 1987

Upon reaching the gravesite, the coffin was placed on two-by-fours that straddled the grave hewn out of red Georgia clay. Murphy read from Psalm 23 and then everyone joined in song:

> There is a balm in Gilead to make the wounded whole.
> There is a balm in Gilead to heal the sin sick soul.
> Sometimes I feel discouraged, and think my work's in vain.
> But then the Holy Spirit revives my soul again.
> If you cannot preach like Peter, if you cannot pray like Paul,
> you can tell of the love of Jesus, and say "He died for all."

After several readings from the Bible, those gathered were invited to share their memories of Joe Mulligan. A woman spoke of his love for the open spaces of the beach and the ocean. She joyfully proclaimed that now, after so many years in prison, he was free to enjoy the beach of heaven. A man read from one of Joe Mulligan's favorite passages in Martin Luther King, Jr.'s book, *Strength to Love:*

> To our most bitter opponents we say: "We shall match your capacity to inflict suffering by our capacity to endure suffering. We shall meet your physical force with soul force. Do to us what you will, and we shall continue to love you. . . . Throw us in jail, and we shall still love you. Send your hooded perpetrators of violence into our community at the midnight hour and beat us and leave us half dead, and we shall still love you. But be ye assured that we will wear you down by our capacity to suffer. One day we shall win freedom, but not only for ourselves. We shall so appeal to your heart and conscience that we shall win in the process, and our victory will be a double victory."

Joe, the man said, applied this passage to his situation on death row, hoping that if he could not be free, his suffering and death would eventually lead people to free others from death sentences. In this way Joe Mulligan fought his own feelings of despair and bitterness while on death row.

As the service closed, members of the Open Door and Jubilee communities stepped forward and using several ropes, slowly lowered the coffin into the grave. Each person who wished to do so took turns with the shovels, lifting the red clay into the tomb. When this task was finished, Joseph Mulligan's mother laid a wreath on the grave and then tearfully stepped away.

The walk back to Koinonia House for dinner was quiet but not despondent. More stories of the life of Joe Mulligan were shared, and the portrait was drawn of a man who could not be simply dismissed as a murderer. The funeral, away from the glare of media and the words of prosecutors and politicians about the necessity of the death penalty for mad killers, witnessed that Joseph Mulligan, too, was a human being, flawed but loved.

The state could, and did, end his life, but it could not restrict his life to its judgment and execution. The state had proclaimed Joseph Mulligan beyond redemption. The stories, prayers, and songs of those gathered under the pines at Jubilee refuted the State's judgment and proclaimed the faith that through Jesus Christ his life was redeemed. In this alternative space, the human dignity of the person who had been killed was affirmed.

In experiences such as this funeral, in letters and visits with prisoners, and in protest, members of the Open Door community find themselves renewed in their faithful, God-inspired struggle for life and liberation consistent with the reign of God. Members of the community find a deep hope emerges out of the suffering and terrible discouragement that comes with each execution. This hope emerges when they gather in prayer and bring their experiences into the context of God's Word. In such times, there is renewal in the belief that their struggle joins with God's struggle for the reign of God.

As is often the case for the community, Matthew 25 serves as a primary scriptural referent. In feeding the hungry and visiting the prisoner, members of the community experience the presence of God. God's presence, the reign of God, brings fullness of life. God opposes the variety of ways in which the powers of sin and death deform and destroy human existence. In Matthew 25, it is evident that to be graciously invited into the reign of God means resisting death through a life given for and with those who are poor, imprisoned, and despised by society. And this resistance includes not only offering soup or visiting in prison, but also working to bring justice. Murphy states:

> It doesn't make sense to serve food or to visit people in prison and come to know them and pray for them and then not cry out on their behalf when their human

> dignity and their very lives are threatened. We are not called to serve without also being called to raise Cain about the humanity and dignity being denied these folks.

It is in the raising of this Cain that the community joins in the liberating life of Jesus Christ and resists death through its practices of visitation and activism on behalf of those imprisoned.

8

FAITH PRACTICES IN THE LIFE OF THE COMMUNITY

IN ITS WORK OF HOSPITALITY, both for those on the streets and in prison, in its work of political activism, and in its shared life in community, the Open Door relies upon and reflects a deep faith. But, what are the major commitments and practices in the faith life of the Open Door Community?

The Open Door in its community life, hospitality, and activism seeks to embody a new way of life that reconciles people, develops relationships of respect and mutuality, and reflects Jesus' mission to bring life, life to the full (John 10:10). A constant refrain in the Open Door is that in Christ a new life begins that entails resistance to the "powers and principalities" and the sins of materialism and consumerism, racism, sexism, heterosexism, and violence and militarism. Living the faith of Jesus brings resistance to these sins that distort our personal lives, and our culture and institutions. These sins separate people from each other, foster domination, and are dehumanizing and destructive.

In the community's structures of membership and authority, and in the practice of hospitality to homeless persons and to persons in prison and on death row, we have seen the Open Door's redemptive concern to build life-giving and joyful relationships. In the next two chapters we will also see ways in which the Open Door extends that redemptive work in seeking the transformation of institutions to bring a more just society. Here we consider how the Open Door's faith practices reflect transformation in Christ—a dying to sin and rising to new life. The community practices solidarity with the poor and simplicity of life to resist the sins of materialism and consumerism. The community practices personalism to undo the sins of racism and all dehumanizing "isms" including heterosexism and sexism. The community practices peacemaking to nonviolently resist economic injustice, the death penalty, and war. All of these faith practices are grounded in worship and prayer that open the heart and mind to see the world from a "God's-eye" perspective, a perspective that comes from the poor—God's presence with the poor.

THE PRESENCE OF GOD WITH THE POOR

To the left of the dining room door at the Open Door hangs a Fritz Eichenberg print called "The Christ of the Breadlines, 1950." Underneath the print is the poem:

> I saw a stranger yestreen,

FRITZ EICHENBERG, "THE CHRIST OF THE BREADLINES, 1950"

I put food in the eating place,
Drink in the drinking place,
Music in the listening place,
And in the name of the blessed Triune,
He blessed my house and myself,
My cattle and my dear ones.
And the lark said in her song:
often, often, often,
The Christ comes in the stranger's guise,
often, often, often,
The Christ comes in the stranger's guise.

We have seen that at the heart of the community's practice of hospitality is the conviction that God's presence is encountered in the poor, the homeless person, and the prisoner. The Open Door draws from liberation theology, the Catholic Worker movement, and the Black struggle for liberation, all of which urge that God sides with the poor. God acts to liberate the downtrodden from oppression and enjoins hospitality for the stranger. Reflecting its association with Dorothy Day and the Catholic Worker movement, the community consistently turns to Matthew 25:31–46 as a key text for its life, along with

Isaiah 58:6–14, Romans 12, and Hebrews 13:1–3. In the homeless and the imprisoned, especially those imprisoned on death row, the Open Door finds Christ.

This is a crucial faith commitment in the community that structures community life. In numerous articles in *Hospitality,* and in conversations with members of the community, the theme is continually present: "in the faces of the stranger and the prisoner we see the face of Jesus Christ." Elizabeth Dede writes:

> The question "Lord, when did we see you?" is a question central to our faith because seeing, recognizing, and understanding are acts of faith as we live in the post-Ascension world. Jesus has left this earth, and we can see him now only with the eyes of faith. Often at the Open Door we read Matthew 25 and ask the question, "Lord, when did we see you?" In the answer to that question . . . we find a clear explanation of our calling and work: to be faithful to the risen Christ, we must feed the hungry, give a drink to the thirsty, receive strangers in our home, give clothes to the naked, take care of the sick, and visit the prisoner.

For the Open Door, the homeless and the imprisoned are sacramental. In those who are marginalized and rejected, God is present in a special way. Ed explains what this means for the community:

> The reality and the presence of God is mediated through the presence and suffering of the poor. So as we live our lives in solidarity with the poor, we are able to discover who God is; and God's reality, changing reality, confronting reality is mediated to our lives and calls us to new life which has two foci: life together in community and servanthood.

Seeing Christ in the homeless person, and in the prisoner, the Open Door affirms their dignity and worth as God's children created in the image of God and sharing in the redemption of Jesus Christ. Murphy emphasizes the centrality of the redemption in the community's understanding of its commitment to those on death row:

> Death row is one more ragged edge of our torn world where we must take a stand for life. It is a matter of worship: worship of the God of Life, the God of Hope, the God of Peace, the God of Redemption. It is not a stand to be taken out of myopic sentimentalism. While people are at times wrongly accused and sentenced to die, death row is not a place where we frequently encounter "innocent suffering." It is a place that pushes us to the depths of our belief in God's redeeming power. We acknowledge with Paul that "we have all sinned and fallen short," and we claim only the power of Christ's redeeming love for our salvation. We claim no less for our sisters and brothers on death row. In so doing we meet the Christ who suffered and died for all of us.

Here it is also evident that the community rejects any sentimentality about the poor, the homeless, or the imprisoned when it affirms that God is present with the poor. Such sentimentality is inadequate because it does not take seriously the evil of which human beings are capable, and does not take seriously the evil that has been inflicted upon the homeless and imprisoned.

Affirming God's presence with the poor empowers the community to confront the strength of evil without acknowledging it as the ultimate power in human life. Such faith does not have an easy optimism about progress and the perfectability of human life. This faith is lived out in the heartbreaking experiences of the Open Door. Murphy writes:

> We are not indulged in the luxurious illusion of "progress." Our friends from the streets are more likely to get older, sicker, and even die than to "get themselves together," get jobs, have their own homes, to—if you will—be "rehabilitated." Of our friends in prison, a few make it out of the cycle of despair and death. Many do not.

And this realism about sin roots the community itself in the graciousness of God, as it is God's love that saves, that makes persons whole, not the work of the community. Murphy states:

> How difficult to hear the word that the Gospel calls us to be failures. After all, what are we to expect when we are invited to follow a homeless wanderer whose best friends were uneducated fisherfolk, prostitutes, and other misfits. It is hard to learn that salvation comes not because our work builds steady progress toward the coming of God's kingdom, but because God is full of love and grace for us and the whole creation. Perhaps one reason that God calls us to love the poor is because the reality of the poor mocks our assumptions about progress and success.

SOLIDARITY WITH THE POOR AND "REDUCING THE DISTANCE"

Through solidarity with the poor the community practices its faith in God's presence with the poor. In this solidarity, community members seek to be aligned with the God of Jesus who became incarnate in a poor man executed by the state; who stands opposed to domination and exploitation, and who

SOUP KITCHEN AT CITY HALL, ATLANTA, FESTIVAL OF SHELTERS, 2005

stands for respect for human dignity and liberation. Solidarity with the poor requires reducing the distance between those with more secure economic resources and the poor.

This reducing of the distance means, first of all, offering hospitality and visiting. "We want" says Ed, "to do what Jesus does: reduce the distance. We want to incarnate the Word into our lives and flesh. So, we feed the hungry and visit the prisoner. A most important step on our journey in faith is to reduce the distance between ourselves and the poor. Herein lies the hope for our personal transformation toward love and justice, toward what Martin Luther King, Jr., called The Beloved Community." Reducing the distance thus requires not only hospitality, but also going to the "holy places" where the poor are met, on the streets, in labor pools, at Grady Hospital, Woodruff Park, soup kitchens, in prison, and on death row.

Reducing the distance also means community members practice simplicity of life and the rejection of consumerism. Members of the community wear donated clothing and receive only a small stipend each week for incidental expenses. Meals come from donated food. Community members eat the same food that they serve to the homeless who come for the breakfast and the soup kitchen. Leisure time is spent reading or in conversation with others or taking a walk. They do not watch television. Alcohol is not available in the house. Smoking is discouraged and those who do smoke must do so outside. The day's rhythm includes times for prayer and work and relaxation.

For those who enter the community from a middle-class lifestyle, there are many challenges in this practice of solidarity with the poor. Food, clothing, and recreation are no longer individual consumer choices. In community one eats what is served, wears what is donated, and recreates without the numbing of television and mass entertainment. It is a way of life that is quite different from the consumer-oriented society. Further, going to the "holy places" to meet those who are poor is jarring. Coming to know people who are poor, learning their stories, seeing the way in which the system is stacked against them, begins to dismantle old ways of seeing the world. Finally, the disciplined way of life coupled with the work and the usual frictions of living together reveal one's own shortcomings (and those of others), and drive one to prayer, to forgiveness, or to leave.

In reducing the distance and coming to solidarity with the poor, community members come to a different perspective on the American way of life. Instead of evaluating society from the position of the powerful who benefit from the current system, the Open Door sees from the position of those who are vulnerable and suffer in this society. Everything the community does is evaluated from the perspective of how it will affect the poor, especially those who are homeless and imprisoned. "Is it good news for the poor?" is the key question for community life. In the same manner, the Open Door advocates that social policy be evaluated according to its affect on the most vulnerable in society. Murphy explains:

> Our vantage point for understanding ourselves and our body politic is to be from the side of the most condemned and despised. It is from the place of the marginalized that we seek understanding of our common values, the basis of our social, political, and economic life and decisions. It is from the perspective of the suffering poor that we come to understand who we are.

Solidarity with the poor, expressed in the discipline of the life of the community, thus brings members to experience the failures and sinfulness of humanity, and at the same time the grace made available to all in Jesus Christ. Whether from the streets, the prisons, or the mainstream of American society, all community members join in the grace-empowered struggle to be free from sin. All in the community seek to live in the new humanity of Christ that puts aside selfishness, addictions, individualism, the many ways in which persons try to survive on their own in this world, and to avoid the emptiness and loneliness of life, and temptations to despair. This recognition of the common nature of the struggle with brokenness opens up the possibility of a mutual welcoming of each other in community. The homeless and the imprisoned are welcomed as fellow human beings embracing the new life of redemption just as those from the mainstream of society.

Ed, in reflecting upon this shared participation in God's liberating redemption, explains the social implications of the Christian doctrine of justification by faith. He provides a corrective to the individualistic interpretations of this doctrine held by many Christians. Justification by faith, he begins, severs our reliance on our works to attain righteousness and salvation. The social ramifications of this belief are clear:

> Since "none are righteous, no not one," no person can say, "I am better." No one can say, "I deserve more because I am more talented, or I have worked harder." No one can say "I am more important because I own more, or I am more educated, or I hold this position in society." Given this radical equality in the eyes of God, we as Christians must avoid erecting barriers, and avoid creating and supporting inequalities of wealth, class, status. We must, if rich, understand that our wealth comes from others and belongs to all who are in need. We must always work against the structures, the institutions in our society that place one above the other in terms of human dignity and worth. We do not all seek to be the same, rather we work to prevent the using of our differences to justify structures of dominance and oppression which place people in categories, and then conclude that people in certain categories do not count.

PERSONALISM

Personalism is a faith practice the Open Door draws primarily from Dorothy Day and the Catholic Worker Movement. Personalism, first of all, affirms each person's human dignity as distinctively created by God in God's image and redeemed by Jesus Christ. Personalism insists that each person be treated with respect and with loving care as a unique child of God. Second, based on that dignity, personalism resists the reduction of human relationships and responsibility to institutional bureaucratic rules and roles. Instead, personalism urges that each of us do what we can to lovingly respond to the needs of others, especially the poor. Murphy wrote of personalism in *Hospitality* back in 1984:

> I like to think that the notion of personalism takes what is best about the graciousness and welcome and attention that lives at the heart of Southern hospitality and applies it upside down: hospitality is particularly—especially—for the least among us. An interest in detail of life leads us to open our eyes to the physical and spiritual detail of the lives of the poor and oppressed, and to see the sufferings of Christ among us. . . . Each person who comes is for us the living Christ. Our love for Jesus makes us restless to see the burden of oppression lifted.

Ed, in the same year, urged that "The life of faith is personal, not organizational or institutional. To be personal, we must find the size which enables us to work hard and rest well, but allows us to love one another, know each other's names, histories, joys and wounds."

The community's commitment to personalism has been tested many times. How to give personal attention to each person's needs when there are so many people in need? In chapter five we saw how the community's struggle over the practice of authority brought an early test of personalism. Murphy remembers that this was not only an issue about authority in the community. It also involved "struggling through the issues around the cheese was a defining moment in our life as a community. It was a time of clarification . . . about the necessary consistency of means and ends." Personalism meant the community would not continue to rely on government supplied cheese because to do so threatened to subsume community hospitality into bureaucratic relations with the homeless.

BREAKFAST AT 910, 2005

Another test of personalism came when some volunteers wanted to make serving in the soup kitchen "more efficient" by posting signs telling people coming in for the meal what they could and could not do. Ruth Allison, a resident volunteer and then a partner in the mid-1980s, explained why posting rules violated personalism:

> We don't just put up signs to organize the soup kitchen. Each person that comes in is greeted and directed to a place at one of the tables. We try to develop relationships with the people we serve. When we pray, it is not about the "homeless problem." The focus instead is on persons; on the needs of individual persons who come to us. This isn't always easy in the face of the numbers who come to our door. And sometimes it would be easier to become angry or depressed or to dismiss someone as a hopeless case.

In contrast to posting signs, community members wear nametags so they can be known by name by those they serve. Also, in recent years photos with the names of those regularly served at the Open Door are posted in the first floor hallway with a banner over the photos that reads, "They are not numbers. They are names."

Some of the harder, more recent tests of the community's commitment to personalism have been the decisions in the past few years to reduce the number of meals and other services. Here the community's greater intentionality about drawing upon the Catholic Worker tradition beginning in the late 1990's was particularly helpful. Murphy explains:

> According to the wisdom of the Worker tradition, when we start trying to expand and do more and more and to do it all more efficiently, we lose the personal relationships on which the Works of Mercy must be based. If we really believe that in the suffering poor we meet the presence of God, then we must avoid mass solutions and the kind of "efficiency" that runs roughshod over the particular voices and needs of individual persons.

At the Open Door, personalism's affirmation of human dignity is also the basis for rejecting racism, sexism and heterosexism. In terms of the latter, the community began to emphasize in the early 1990's the welcome of gays and lesbians. Ed wrote of this development in an August 2000 *Hospitality* article. "We are learning new ways to read the Bible and to practice the radical love ethic of welcome and inclusion from the heart that is revealed by Jesus Christ." He connected this welcoming with the welcoming of Gentiles into the early church. "What the early followers of Jesus did for us non-Jews is now the task at hand for us to do for gays and lesbians." Ed expressed hope that in both church and society, "Our brothers who are gay and our sisters who are lesbians will, someday soon we pray, be accorded the same welcome and the same love, dignity and membership that God in infinite mercy has bestowed on each one of us."

A long-standing expression of personalism at the Open Door is the commitment to feminism. Women in the Open Door Community share equally in decision-making, and in the crucial daily roles of authority such as house duty, leading the soup kitchen, the breakfast, the shower line, and worship. This same equality is affirmed in the language of the community. Inclusive language is used in worship. "References to women," an early community resolution stated, "should not belittle or exploit but rather build up and reflect reality. Women are women, not girls, or ladies, or sweethearts, or babies." Responding to a letter from a man upset at the inclusive language used in *Hospitality* which referred to God as "She," Ed wrote:

> In our desire to be faithful to the God of the Bible and end the reign of patriarchy, we find it most helpful that God is neither male nor female. There are Biblical references and analogies to God as mother and she, therefore, we have decided to use a language inclusive of God as mother and God as woman. This does not mean that we do not refer to God as father, or God as he, but it does mean that we want to be open to the new experiences of God as more light is always breaking forth from the word of God. . . . In this way we believe we can contribute to breaking down the dividing walls of sexism, as Jesus Christ has done before us and for us. . . . It is our aim and purpose to be about the work of dismantling patriarchy. As you well know, we are also in a struggle against racism, classism, the roles of prisons, labor pools and homelessness in our society. All of this is one piece. The aim and purpose is to continue to follow Jesus as we move our feet towards the Beloved Community. . . .

The Open Door understands the exclusion of women from full participation in all areas of life as oppressive and enslaving. Women historically have been denied the freedom "to enjoy the fullness of life that God promises us through Jesus Christ." Since Christ acts to bring reconciliation among all people and with God, the Open Door seeks with Christ the full inclusion of women in its community life. This involves not only including female terms in relation to God, but also remaking assumed roles for women and men. In Christ there is the call to be a new man and a new woman. For the new man, the challenge is to reject "macho" views and to practice tenderness, listening, and service to others. For the new woman, the challenge is to reject patriarchy and to practice leadership, interdependence rather than dependence, and service without subservience.

The personalist commitment to respect each other as made in the image of God supports efforts to challenge any person who denies the dignity due to women. When a homeless man during the offering of showers continued to refer to a female resident volunteer as "honey," Ira, who was leading the giving of showers, challenged him: "Her name is Lauren." This kind of mutual support reflects the community's commitment to the dignity of each as a person.

Another aspect of personalism is that community members must, in the words of Gandhi, "be the change they wish to see" in the larger society; there must be a unity of ends and means. Ed quotes evangelical theologian Ron Sider who says, "Don't ask the government or culture to do anything you are not already doing in your synagogue, mosque, and church." This leads to the recognition that the sin confronted in the larger society resides within one's own heart, and so the transformation urged for the society must also be reflected in one's own life. As we saw in our discussion of membership and authority, the Open Door sees its internal tensions and conflicts as part of the larger struggle for the Beloved Community. The community confesses its sin and continues to call upon God in prayer for the liberating transformation promised in Christ. Ed writes:

> Our Beloved Communities will always be made up of twisted vessels—sinners in our life together—as we are every day at the Open Door Community. One cost of diversity and liberation is that we sin more often. . . . At home, in our house of hospitality, we are a community of the guilty, the condemned. . . . We are desperate and starving for a new way, a new covenant, a revolutionary forgiveness and a forgiving revolution.

Personalism is also manifested in the community's attention to the relation between the works of mercy and the work for justice. Both are ways to express respect for human dignity. Ed explains that the community, "resists the split within the camp of the socially concerned between those who seek to aid hurting persons and others who fight to change the systems of abuse and injustice." He calls this split "the charity-justice polarity, or the band-aids versus root causes approach." There is an ongoing tension in the life of the community between the need for more direct service to the poor, and political advocacy to address the structures of injustice that create this need. But Ed finds this is a necessary and creative tension. From activities such as "sleeping with the homeless, eating with the hungry, waiting with the convicted, putting a band-aid on an open sore, that create wonderful friendships, comes the energy for the long haul battle with the powers and principalities of death." He says, "The anger and hurt and pain that we experience with and on behalf of homeless persons and on behalf of prisoners is, of course, alleviated most quickly through direct action [of works of mercy]. But we need to take our anger and insight and become more engaged in the political and social arenas."

The Open Door sees the exploitation of the poor by the powerful grounded in utilitarian and social contract approaches to human life that deny human dignity. The economy and the political order institutionally express these forms of individual self-interest. Social critic Philip Slater in *The Pursuit of Loneliness* describes how this institutionalized individualism supports what he calls the "Toilet Assumption" in American culture. Instead of recognizing our interdependence as persons in community, we deny responsibility for others and seek to solve social problems by flushing them out of sight. The old, the poor, the mentally unbalanced, and minorities are placed in "institutional holes where they cannot be seen." When these sewers back up, a "special commission" is formed to investigate the problem and propose solutions. The solutions inevitably suggest new institutional holes (a better toilet) or fine tuning those that already exist (fix the plumbing). Since the commission members are drawn from those who profit from the system, it is never fundamentally challenged. Rather than address the need for institutional change, the toilet assumption regards poverty as purely individual failure. As *Atlanta Journal-Constitution* newspaper columnist Dick Williams put it in the late 1980's, homelessness is primarily "an individual problem, not a capitalist system run amok. We have individuals who drink and snort [cocaine] and forsake all responsibility."

Treatment of the homeless in our society reflects how the toilet assumption works. Numerous task forces and commissions on homelessness have been formed, and new bureaucracies created and staffed by professionals, to address the "problem." None of these suggest any fundamental transformation of the economic system based upon self-interest. None of these even urge the necessity of the city meeting the basic human need for toilets where as Ed says, people could "pee for free with dignity." Capitalism remains in place, and thus the assumptions remain that the poor are the problem, rather than the way our society is structured. Ed thus observes, "I just don't think the way you help the poor is by playing with the rich. It's one of the myths of democratic society that insures the further development of the middle class. I think one thing that is lacking in our society is a recognition that one of the root causes of poverty is—wealth."

The Open Door's commitment to personalism also means its theological and political analysis is rooted in solidarity with the poor. Mark Harper, a former resident volunteer who spent twenty-four hours on the streets, sought to view things from the perspective of the poor. He stayed part of the night with a few homeless people who sought shelter in a crawl space under the First National Bank Tower in downtown Atlanta. He described the bank building as symbolic of the national values of the pursuit of wealth and security. He urged that being in the crawl space

> provides a much better lens through which to view the reality of our world than, say, any one of the windows of the tall buildings that rise around it. In fact, is there not an inherent danger that people will be pulled away from a necessary sense of our brokenness when they become engaged in the enterprise of any institution (from banks to a great many churches) that offers competition as a primary frame of reference?

Mark saw both the brokenness of individuals who are homeless and the brokenness of the system that denies our need for each other. Individual responsibility and institutional arrangements must be addressed together. As Peter Maurin who founded the Catholic Worker with Dorothy Day said, "We must create a society in which it is easier for people to be good." As long as individual competition remains a fundamental value, the recognition of our shared need for healing and the consequent moral imperative to transform social systems to heal the vulnerable will be lacking. The toilet assumption will continue to work.

The Open Door also finds the toilet assumption at work with the poor and African Americans who end up in disproportionate numbers in prison and on death row. Execution, of course, is the ultimate toilet. Society attempts to flush away those it considers crap, those seen as beyond redemption. Like the homeless who are treated as non-persons, the prisoner on death row is de-personalized. Prosecutors and the media portray those on death row as crazed animals who deserve to die. Through the routine of prison life and its rituals of degradation, prisoners are daily reminded that society regards them as deserving of neither respect nor care.

The Open Door, in contrast, affirms that it is the specific task of Christians to witness to the God-given dignity of all persons both by how the poor are treated and by efforts to transform society. In a *Hospitality* article titled, "All God's Children Gotta Have Shoes," Ed gave an eloquent summation of this shared life as he reflected on the feet of Lonnie Moss. Lonnie had been invited into the community from the streets. Now he was in the hospital, dying of cancer. As Ed sat at the end of the hospital bed, he noticed Lonnie's feet deformed from years of bad shoes and neglect. Such deformation of the feet of a person made in God's image, Ed wrote, was not part of God's intention for the world. With this in mind, he outlined how redemption reasserts the intention of God in creation, while as judge, God continues to resist injustice:

> That "all God's children got shoes" is a vision of hope, a prayer for the coming of Thy Kingdom on earth as it is in heaven! Shoes are not only necessary items for survival and health; shoes are also symbols of human dignity and social justice. Until each of us has warm,

> dry, and comfortable shoes, the feet of God shall ache. Where there are those without good shoes, there is injustice in the system and deep terrible pain among those who suffer shoelessness.

The Open Door, in practicing personalism, seeks justice by making public the right to shoes while also practicing love by providing shoes now as part of its hospitality for the homeless.

PEACEMAKING: NONVIOLENT RESISTANCE TO INJUSTICE AND STATE KILLING

The Open Door's commitment to nonviolence calls upon the witness of Jesus and the early church, St. Benedict, St. Francis and St. Clare, Anabaptists and Quakers, Dorothy Day and the Catholic Worker Movement, Martin Luther King, Jr., Fannie Lou Hamer, Cesar Chavez, Daniel and Philip Berrigan, and a host of others. The Open Door is emphatic: to kill another human being is contrary to the gospel of Jesus Christ. Murphy Davis states, "Our vocation as Christians is always to stand as witnesses to life. We must be about the tasks of healing and restoration rather than revenge and further violence." Ed says, "We are to be known as Jesus' disciples by the way we love each other in the peace of God."

The community knows of state violence firsthand as many of those executed by the state of Georgia were friends of community members who visited them on death row. The conviction of the community is that God's redeeming love must break the cycle of violence. The community's peacemaking should be understood not only as a political method, but as integral to their moral vision and way of life. Peacemaking as a way of life includes self-examination to uncover the violence harbored within, even as it demands involvement in nonviolent struggle for justice.

Within the community this self-examination and attention to the violence within can emerge from the experience of living together.

Lauren Cogswell saw this in her life when, on house duty one day, she asked some volunteers from the streets to move to a different table during lunch because the community expects people to sit together during common meals. The volunteers got angry with her. She reflected that she could have addressed the issue differently by going to sit with them and to invite others to do the same. She saw later that, "Sometimes when you're on house duty it's really hard. You've got so many things going on and you just want to solve things. So the first kind of instinctual reaction is, 'you can't do that; you need to move.' Which is usually my first reaction instead of thinking of a creative solution." At other times community members are regularly called to practice peacemaking in response to anger, threats, and physical violence that sometimes comes when the hurt of the streets boils over into the breakfast, soup kitchen, or showers. Community members seek to "not be overcome by evil but overcome evil with good" (Romans 12:21) and to defuse volatile situations. As Mike Reese, a former resident of the community who came from the streets said one morning when he was cursed at while he was serving breakfast, "I responded with humility. I would have never acted this way before, but I'm trying to love, to follow Jesus. I said I was sorry and walked away."

In resisting their own tendencies to violence, the community also resists the larger culture, including many Christians who endorse and participate in violence. Ed, in seeing so much Christian support for war and the death penalty, has taken to emphasizing the newness of what God did (and does) in Jesus Christ. As he imaginatively depicts God's decision to move from the Old to the New Covenant, he intertwines peacemaking with God's presence among the poor and solidarity with the poor:

> Yahweh got ready for the central event and greatest change in all of human history. . . . God would call this second phase "The New Covenant." It would reveal a new way and a new content. First Yahweh-Elohim said, "I am going to come and dwell among these people myself. The Word must become flesh!". . . . People would finally "see God" and learn how to live the truth. Second, violence had failed, just as words had failed. God decided that the flesh must be an instrument of peace. Taking a big step, Yahweh said, "We must love our enemies and bless those who curse us. In fact, I shall call the peacemakers my daughters and my sons.". . . . Third, God said that the new covenant would turn the order of things upside down. "I'm tired of David's doings with power and might and the building of empire and big temples. It just don't work. God decided then and there to be born poor, stay poor, and in the flesh always be poor. Yahweh-Elohim changed David's messianic vision from kings and courts to outcasts and disposable people. "If you want to find me, you gotta hit the streets and barns.". . . . Finally, this New Covenant of flesh and blood will be one of bread and drink, at the supper table where all are called to come and practice nonviolent love, to embody a life of solidarity with the poor.

Consistent with this vision of God as peacemaker, the Open Door throughout its history has used the pages of *Hospitality* to urge resistance to war-making. The community has offered resistance not only to the death penalty, but also to the MX missile, to nuclear weapons build-up, to U.S. support of dictators and terrorism in Latin America, Asia, Africa, and the Middle East. The community regularly participates in the demonstrations for peace, including the annual demonstration against the School of the Americas (SOA) at Ft. Benning, Georgia. Extended friends of the community such as Toni Flynn and Don Beisswenger have been imprisoned for their resistance to the SOA. The community practices war tax resistance. In the last few years, community members have spoken out and acted against the war in Iraq, with many articles in *Hospitality* detailing the faith reasons for opposition to this war and all war.

PRAYER AND ACTIVISM

Prayer is central to the life of the Open Door. Anthony Eunice, a former community member from the streets, puts it bluntly:

> I don't think this community life could exist in the manner and in the concreteness that it does without prayer life. The spirituality part of this community I really believe gives the Open Door its sense of direction. I've not seen the magnitude of love in any context or organization or any group of people like I've seen here. I don't think folks can fake that. Prayer and spirituality here is the ground that holds our relationships together.

The gracious power of God sustains the community's commitment to liberation and to the creation of the beloved community. In God's loving grace, community members are transformed. The experience of God present with the poor leads to solidarity, hospitality, and resistance to injustice. Prayer and worship express this faith and nurture it.

In an early interview with a local Catholic paper, Ed echoed the advice of Thomas Merton to activists:

> To allow oneself to be carried away by a multitude of demands, to commit oneself to too many projects, to

> want to help everyone in everything is to succumb to violence. The frenzy of the activist neutralizes his or her work for peace. It destroys the fruitfulness of his of her work because it kills the root of inner wisdom which makes work fruitful.

The way to prevent this kind of activism, Ed explained, is to keep one's activism grounded in prayer:

> The activism of the community must be rooted in spiritual discipline. Work with the poor which is not spiritually based can lead to hatred of the poor; patronizing the poor. In the pressure of the activist life, the first thing you give up is prayer. One reason I advocate community life together is so we may be alone with God. Thus the community's covenant states "As sisters and brothers we covenant to submit to a daily discipline based on scripture and prayer."

In prayer, the community encounters God, and in this relationship the love necessary for personal relationships with the homeless or with prisoners is nourished. Jodi Garbison, a resident volunteer, puts it simply, "Prayer keeps me from getting numb and callous." Ed speaks to the necessity of this love:

> In the absence of love, and in specialization, people become objects—objects of our specialty. Marx's insight about the worker being alienated from their work can be applied here. When we become alienated from our work, what we produce is seen only as an object over against us. In the same way, I could see the poor only as objects to be manipulated, and so come to despise the very people I hope to love.

Prayer renews the community in the love of God which makes possible love for each other and for the stranger. As Murphy puts it:

> What we give is rooted in love because of God's hospitality for us. We are not a social service agency. We all are on the receiving end. We are all outsiders made into community, family, friends through Jesus Christ. The basis for this is seen in Second Corinthians where Paul writes that through Jesus all enemies are made friends of God. Friendship comes from God. We don't give that friendship, but receive it and share it. Then in Matthew 25 we read that when we feed the hungry, we feed Jesus Christ. The way we treat the dirtiest, hungriest, smelliest, drunkest person is the way we treat God.

For community members the practice of daily prayer is considered crucial. Tony Sinkfield, who came to the community from the streets, recalls that "Prior to being here I really didn't have a spiritual life. I didn't realize how important it is to start my day off right with bible reading and meditation. Being aware that I need to do these things has been really helpful." Gladys Rustay echoes Tony, "Worship and prayer are essential. If I have a hard day I know I missed prayer."

As a Protestant Catholic Worker house, the Open Door has practiced from its beginning a rich liturgical life that reflects a Catholic sacramentality. From the outset the community has celebrated the Lord's Supper every Sunday. Murphy identifies this worship as "the center of our life." Nelia Kimbrough, a partner in the community, explains, "We are a Eucharistic community and that is where the ultimate authority rests. It's what gathers us together, what sustains us in our brokenness, what grounds us in the work." The Sunday Eucharist is celebrated in the dining room where homeless persons are served

MAUNDY THURSDAY, HOLY WEEK ON THE STREETS, 2005

meals and the community has its meals. It includes not only the community members, but regular volunteers, and persons from the streets. There is singing, time for sharing "prayer concerns," for preaching, and for the sharing of the bread and the cup. Immediately following the service, everyone present is invited to share in a feast with the community.

The community also attends to the traditional liturgical calendar of the Christian faith. Murphy explains why this is important:

> The Christian liturgical year is meant to rehearse for us again and again the drama of faith: the drama of God's merciful action on our behalf. We are slow to learn and so we must go over and over to appropriate the radical depth of the Gospel life. Always the struggle is to bring to bear how we encounter God's action and the cry of the poor in our particular context. And so the year is shaped.

However, unlike most mainline churches, the Open Door draws out the political and economic dimensions of this liturgical remembering, and also has added seasonal liturgical events particularly tied to the community's convictions. The liturgy itself thus becomes a place of resistance to the values and practices of the dominant society. Ed states:

> The American way of life has absorbed and domesticated the particularity of a biblical and Christian witness. This is most clearly observed around Christmas, Easter, and when the state of Georgia crucifies a death row brother. For those of us in the family of faith and the household of hope, it does not have to be that way. We can refuse and resist. We can find other public expressions of our inward faith. ... Over the years, we at the Open Door Community have sought liturgical expressions for our faith and way of life that point to the character of our God.

Those liturgical expressions include foot washing, Advent, Lent and Holy Week on the Streets, and the Festival of Shelters in the Public Arena.

Traditionally practiced by many Christian churches on the Thursday of Holy Week, the Open Door's practice of foot washing has become an important sacramental remembering and renewing of their service to one another in the community. The Open Door affirms the connection of foot washing with the Eucharist, celebrating this practice during the Lord's Supper shared during community retreats at Dayspring farm. Elizabeth reflected on the spiritual renewal she experienced in one such retreat, "As we rest and recreate together, share the Lord's Supper, and wash each other's feet, then we remember and experience and are conscious of Christ, the bright Dayspring, shining on us and sharing both the joy and the bitter sadness of our hearts."

The community also recalls in the foot washing the community's Thursday night foot clinic, just as the breakfast and the soup kitchen are connected with the community's celebration of the Eucharist. The bringing together of sacramental renewal in service with joyful celebration is evident in the foot washing which inevitably elicits smiles as community members alternate receiving and giving of the foot washing. A few community members remember when Gabriel Cole-Vodicka, a baby at the time, sat down by the water and splashed himself from head to toe with great delight. Someone suggested that perhaps he felt like Peter who had told Jesus: "Lord, do not wash only my feet, then! Wash my hands and head, too."

The community's celebration of Advent resists the commercialization of Christmas. This season begins with a community retreat. Community members recall the Christmas story in its full political and economic dimensions—a child said to be a king yet born in a barn and pursued by Herod who seeks his death. This is also a time in the community where the harsh realities of the cold weather for homeless people provide a sharp contrast between the values of our capitalistic economic system and the call of Jesus to serve the poor.

Lent begins for the community with an Ash Wednesday service held early in the morning. Psalm 51, a powerful confession of sin and hope for redemption provides the central prayer for worship. The community gathers in the back yard at 910 where there are memorials to homeless persons who have died on the streets. Community members place in a soup pot a small piece of paper upon which they have written the sin they particularly want to repent of during Lent. The paper is burned. Community members in turn use those ashes to make a sign of the cross on the forehead of each member, saying "Remember that you are dust and to dust you shall return." Dick Rustay offers that the symbolism here is that each community members bears the sins of the others during this season, offering support for each other in their efforts at repentance.

Holy Week and the Festival of Shelters, as we saw in chapter six, pull together the heartache and joy of the community's work of hospitality with the homeless. These are special times of remembering the connections between the work of hospitality, advocacy for justice, and the Gospel.

In addition to following the liturgical calendar, the Open Door has daily times for prayer. As we saw in the chapter on hospitality with the homeless, regular times for biblical reflection came to be integrated with serving meals. But there is also time for prayer as the Open Door has sought to bring into rhythm prayer and work.

Mike Vosburg-Casey, a former resident volunteer, tells the story of a person visiting the Open Door who said that it is the "prayingist" community that he has ever seen. He said he was there for one day and he participated in four times of community prayer. After serving the breakfast, before the soup kitchen, and before lunch and supper, members of the community form a circle and join their hands in prayer. Prior to serving others, members of the community remind each other whom it is they serve. It is Christ in the guise of the poor. For this opportunity to serve Christ in the poor, thanks is given. Often there are also prayers for strength or patience or compassion. These come out of experiences in which tempers flared or violence threatened in the serving lines. When you face someone who is angry at being hungry and homeless, it is not always easy to see Christ in that person.

The period of prayer before community meals is a time to share scripture, concerns, and thanks for the good of the day. Community members draw strength from persons in the "extended" community, like Barbara Schenk and Horace Tribble, who persistently and eloquently share prayer concerns with and for the community. C. M. Sherman, who had come from the streets and became a partner in the community, explains further:

> Members can assemble daily to call upon each other to share concerns, sorrows, burdens, and weaknesses, while calling upon the Lord to intervene and help shape our lives. It is a measure to attain a quality of life of joy through commitment to the Gospel, and to resist not only the sins of the world, but also the sins of our individual selves. We attempt to nullify the effects of those divisions of race, class, and background through working, sharing, and playing together. We hope for mutuality in Christ.

For Elizabeth Dede the informal prayer of the Open Door was initially difficult for her. Raised as a Lutheran, she remembers her hesitation with this prayer:

> As a House Duty person, I was expected to take prayer concerns and say prayers out loud. I was very nervous doing this because I had no experience saying prayers that weren't found in a book. At the Open Door, prayer takes on an immediate quality that didn't exist in those traditional, printed prayers of my childhood. I've never been able to find a prayer for blue jeans for the clothes closet in the *Book of Common Prayer.*

For others who come to the community, there is also learning in what it means to pray. Heather Bargeron, a former resident volunteer, reflected that for her prayer has been "a touchy issue." She has struggled to pray, saying that before coming to the Open Door "I just couldn't really get interested in developing an individual prayer life, and most of the time I didn't really see the need for regular prayer." She came to see that "as a white middle-class kid growing up in the suburbs, I simply was not in the right location to experience God's intervention on earth nor to see a real need for prayer on a regular basis for myself or for anybody in my immediate surroundings." At the Open Door, her experiences with the suffering of the homeless and imprisoned, her own sense of limitations in trying to address that suffering, and the persistence of the evil made prayer a necessity for both personal and social transformation. "If we truly pray," she stated, "for God's transformation in our hearts and community, we must work daily for God's way of justice and peace." She continued, "We do not pray out of some vague hope that some day God will heal this messed up world while we sit back and watch in amazement. We are called to live our prayers and to pray for our lives." In prayer, she concludes, "God empowers us, the faithful, to save one another from the powers of death and to redeem one another through our prayers, our work, and our living out an alternative to the powers in our everyday lives. As we pray and we become more aligned with the character of God, we are moved to participate in the works of justice."

VIGIL AT CENTRAL CITY (NOW WOODRUFF) PARK, ATLANTA, 1984

9

FAITHFUL RESISTANCE IN RESPONSE TO HOMELESSNESS

IN ATLANTA, AS IN MOST OTHER MAJOR CITIES IN THE UNITED STATES, those who control economic and political power hold to a fundamental belief, "Whatever benefits the central business district benefits everyone." This belief is often expressed in development projects funded in part or whole through various forms of taxpayer dollars and/or tax abatements by which developers are exempted from property taxes. It is also expressed in continuous efforts to clear the streets of homeless and other poor people through laws that, in effect, criminalize poverty. The use of laws and police pressure to clear the streets exposes the contradiction in the belief. Whatever benefits the central business district does not benefit everyone. Instead, it benefits those who profit from such development, while it further criminalizes the homeless, and at best creates a few more low-paying service-sector jobs for the poor. In Atlanta, there has been a remarkable consistency by business and political powers to put forth and enforce their belief. These powers criminalize the poor through the absence of public toilets, police sweeps of parks as part of an establishment of "vagrant-free zones"; laws against "urban camping" and panhandling, and other "quality of life" ordinances.

The Open Door, from its start, connected its practice of hospitality to resistance of such policies. In practicing hospitality the community sees how the suffering of the homeless is tied into institutional powers. The Open Door has been stubbornly persistent in its efforts to expose how these powers plan and act to exclude the poor. At the same time, the community offers alternatives that would serve and empower the poor. The practice of redemptive hospitality in works of mercy leads the community to works of justice, in particular the truth-telling that challenges the existing order. Ed bluntly states the community's position, "It is a worldly lie of devastating proportions, violence, dehumanization—yes, a crucifying of our God, a sacrilege as terrible as goddamn—to name a human being created in the likeness of God, redeemed by the blood of our Lord Jesus Christ, a bum."

In the late 1970s and early 1980s, the numbers of homeless persons in Atlanta reached a level where government and business leaders began to consider homelessness a public problem. The *Atlanta Journal* and the *Atlanta Constitution,* in a series of articles about the homeless, defined the business and economic powers' view of the "problem" of homelessness. The articles depicted "derelicts" harassing shoppers and business people in the downtown area. One headline read, "Atlantans Urged to File

Reports On Bums, Punks" and reported that Central Atlanta Progress, an association of downtown business leaders, urged "downtown businesses to have their employees fill out harassment incident reports." The ruling elite equated the homeless to "trash" and saw the homeless as a threat rather than as human beings in need. Another headline read, "City Officials Move to Clear Derelicts from Atlanta Parks." Shortly thereafter, another article reported that park sprinklers would be turned on after 11:00 P.M. until 1:00 A.M. "to make the ground too wet for sleeping."

Even as the night shelter at Clifton was in its infancy in January of 1980, the struggle began to resist these attitudes and actions and instead urge both compassion and justice for the homeless in respect of their dignity as human beings. In a letter to the editor from January 22, 1980, Ed stated:

> These men, excluded by our social system, broken by their personal histories, and pushed from nowhere to nowhere by people who wish not to be bothered, are again the recipients of verbal abuse and planned harassment by the newspapers and the business establishment.

Dan Sweat, the president of Central Atlanta Progress, gave a caustic response to Ed's letter. Calling Ed's approach "myopic and simplistic," Sweat contended the problem of homelessness would "require a lot more from our religious institutions than a placebo theology which equates 'love thy neighbor' with an occasional hot meal, a crash pad, two verses of 'The Old Rugged Cross' and 25 cents for a one way MARTA ride back downtown."

From the early 1980s to the present, the powers have continued to regard the homeless as a threat, and the city's political and business elite have implemented the "Central

Atlanta Plan." Low-income housing has been virtually eliminated. Interstates or other major roadways and construction have isolated or eliminated low income African American neighborhoods from downtown, and upper income housing continues to be built up. All of these developments have helped to increase homelessness and to increase pressure to eliminate homeless and other low-income people, primarily African Americans, from downtown. From the standpoint of the political and economic elite, there are still too many homeless people who congregate each day in high-profile places downtown, such as Woodruff Park in the central business district. These homeless persons, again mostly African American, are regarded as threatening the downtown renaissance powered by attracting more white tourists, residents, and white-owned businesses downtown.

Meanwhile, much of the city's religious leadership avoided addressing social injustice by continuing a traditional Southern emphasis on personal salvation and good manners. The political and economic dynamics of Atlanta reflect those of other major Southern cities. African Americans claimed more political power, but white corporate power continued to exert economic control of the city. The city government, dominated by African Americans, has alternated between seeking to please white business interests and not alienating black voters, many of whom remain poor. In seeking to retain and attract additional businesses downtown, there is a great deal of sensitivity surrounding the downtown area and its image. This sensitivity intensified as efforts were made to attract major sporting and convention events (such as the 1996 Olympics, which coincided with the opening of a big new city jail), and to draw higher income residents downtown as gentrification reversed the flow to the suburbs.

Not surprisingly, proposals to eliminate homeless people from the downtown area continued to be expressed into the new century. When Mayor Shirley Franklin announced plans in the summer of 2003 for a new campaign to "clean-up" downtown, a large picture in the *Journal-Constitution* showed a police officer rousting a homeless woman sleeping on a bench in Woodruff Park. The Mayor's plan and the picture indicated that Central Atlanta Plan's myth that "whatever benefits the central business district benefits everyone" and criminalizing the poor would continue to dominate city responses to the homeless. The National Homeless Civil Rights Organizing Project listed Atlanta as the second meanest city in the nation in relation to the treatment of homeless persons in 2004. In 2005 the city again sought ways to criminalize homeless people through a series of proposed panhandling ordinances. Again the community resisted, organizing protests and engaging in civil disobedience which led to seven community members being jailed.

While the political and economic elite remain determined to eliminate homeless people from downtown, mostly through increased police harassment and arrests, the Open Door remains steadfast in articulating and acting upon an alternative vision. In their political actions, the Open Door and others involved with the poor and homeless in Atlanta confront the myth expressed by city government and business organizations. The business and political elite want an Atlanta in which the poor are made invisible—are "flushed away," so to deny their existence and any responsibility for their well-being. The Open Door seeks what Martin Luther King, Jr., called "the beloved community" in which the human dignity of all persons is affirmed and embodied in racial harmony and economic justice. Here just a few of these struggles are detailed.

THE CAMPAIGN FOR PUBLIC TOILETS, 1983–PRESENT

In the early 1980s, the Open Door joined with other advocates to try and educate city and business officials and churches about homelessness and the needs of homeless people for housing, medical care (including help to end addictions), education, and job training. The Open Door played an important role in helping to create organizations such as Atlanta Advocates for the Homeless. One of the pressing needs the Open Door and such organizations sought to have the city address was public toilets. The reality, then as now, is that homeless persons are constantly arrested on charges of public urination, while the city refuses to provide public restrooms. In a public hearing on the issue at City Hall on October 12, 1983, Rob Johnson from the Open Door asked the city to halt arrests for public urination until public restrooms were provided. He cited figures indicating that over one hundred arrests were made each month on these charges. Since homeless persons could not pay the fines they ended up serving time at the city's work farm. The arrests criminalized people who had no other choice but public urination. At the same public hearing, Dan Sweat of Central Atlanta Progress expressed his worry that if the city had public toilets homeless people from around the nation would flock to Atlanta. He further suggested that the lack of toilets for the homeless was not an insult to their human dignity since by being on the streets homeless persons indicated their own lack of self-respect.

The Open Door and other community activists began to demonstrate and leaflet at City Hall in support of public toilets. At the same time, they pressured the city to open shelters for the homeless. On December 1, 1983, the Open Door held an all night vigil on the steps of City Hall. The city council met the next day and approved the installation of a portable toilet at what was then Plaza Park downtown (it has now been subsumed by Underground Atlanta). Plaza Park was a narrow strip of green near the Five Points Metropolitan Atlanta Rapid Transit Authority (MARTA) station where police generally left homeless persons alone. The council also approved the opening of one emergency shelter for the homeless. A partial victory had been won, but the Open Door clearly saw how inadequate the response of the city continued to be in terms of the needs of the homeless. Ed Loring told the *Atlanta Journal-Constitution*, "The vote represents an unwillingness by this administration to face poverty in our downtown."

In 1984, the Open Door focused on the city's day labor center on Edgewood Avenue. Here was one place where homeless people had access to a bathroom. Federal funds had been allocated in 1983 to renovate and repair the bathrooms. A year later the work had still not begun. The Open Door agitated for the work to begin. Pickets and leafleting yielded no results. By June of 1985 the work had still not begun. The community decided a more dramatic demonstration was needed at City Hall. On June 8th they carried a toilet into Mayor Andrew Young's office and Ed sat on it reading the scriptures. He vowed that he would refuse to move until a contract was signed for the renovation of the labor center. He and two others with him (Will Coleman, a professor at Columbia Seminary) and Dick Stewart (a retired Wycliff Bible Translator) were arrested for disorderly conduct. Their point, however, had been made. Ed's arrest came at noon and by 2 P.M. that afternoon a contract had been signed for the renovation. The construction at the labor center began June 18. The community itself had been renting a portable toilet for use by homeless folks in the community's backyard. This eventually proved unworkable and the community had a public restroom built into the side of the building at 910.

The city of Atlanta has continued to the present to refuse to install public restrooms in the downtown area. A plan to install public toilets for the Olympics was never carried out, and this despite yet another protest with people sitting in with toilets in Mayor Bill Campbell's office in June of 1996. Ed's call for public toilets so that people are able "to pee for free with dignity" has gone unheeded by the city. The campaign continues today with some twenty plus organizations supporting the campaign for public toilets.

Murphy sees the race and class dynamics in the unwillingness of the city to offer public toilets:

> An ugly fact about our society is that many white people still don't want to share bathrooms with people of color. And middle class and wealthy people don't want to share toilets with the poor. There is still a feeling around the city that if we do anything that might help the homeless poor, there will automatically be more of them. So rather than risk that, we allow our public spaces to be inhospitable to everyone.

THE CAMPAIGN FOR 910, 1985–1986

The continued existence of the community itself at 910 was the focus of public controversy through 1985 and 1986. An October 31, 1985, article in the *Atlanta Constitution* purported to describe how efforts in the city to serve the growing homeless population were increasing tensions in areas of the city where the numbers of homeless were especially visible. E. Marcus Davis, a lawyer whose firm occupied the building next to the Open Door was quoted as saying, "Everyday they [the Open Door] serve two meals, and you'll have 50 disheveled-looking people lying around in the yard. At times it looks like a scene from Dante's Inferno. It's just unsightly." According to the article, the law firm wanted the Open Door to move its shower and soup kitchen lines from the front to the back door of its building. The Open Door refused on the grounds that to do so would further stigmatize the homeless as social outcasts and remove them from public awareness.

Eventually the tension between the Open Door and the law firm was mediated with help from Ed Grider of the Atlanta Presbytery. The Open Door agreed to landscape the front yard. Bushes around the edge of the front yard and benches created a gathering space for homeless persons waiting to come into the building for meals or other services. The Open Door remained committed to serving people through the front door of the building. The community also created a gathering space with benches in the backyard, along with a fence. The relations with members of the law firm improved so much so that Marcus Davis became a supporter of the Open Door expressing his admiration for the work the community does. "It is not easy work. They provide a valuable service, especially with the political situation today with policies directed at harming both the poor and the middle class." He described the original article in the *Atlanta Constitution* as a "set up" in which his comments were taken out of context.

As this controversy ended, the neighborhood around the Open Door was involved in a process of gentrification that has continued to the present. The nearby Virginia-Highlands area has seen an influx of young professionals who have renovated older homes. On Ponce de Leon, old structures have been renovated or torn down and new businesses and up-scale residences have been built. An abandoned Ford plant became an upscale shopping center and apartment complex. The neighborhood changed even as it remained "home" for many homeless people.

The *Journal-Constitution*'s attempt to promote a struggle between the law firm and the Open Door prefigured on a small scale the political context in which the Open Door has fought. Government and business leaders, with the help of the city's main newspaper, continually try to portray the homeless as a threat, while also denying any connection between government and business actions and the existence of homelessness in Atlanta. The Open Door and its supporters, including many drawn from their neighborhood, see this fear-mongering about homeless persons as part of a larger pattern of denying human dignity. As long as homeless persons are viewed as a threat to the community, or as somehow less than human, it becomes possible to deny any common obligations to them as members of the human community.

THE CAMPAIGN FOR AL SMITH PARK AND AGAINST THE "VAGRANT-FREE ZONE" AND UNDERGROUND ATLANTA, 1987–1996

In 1987, reflecting the myth of "what's good for the downtown business is what's good for everyone," both city and business officials promoted the image of the homeless as either threats to the good order of the community or as society's losers who deserved life on the streets. Supporting the position of city government and business was the Central Area Study commissioned by the city of Atlanta, Fulton County, and Central Atlanta Progress. The study found the presence of homeless persons in downtown a threat to public safety on both counts and suggested the creation of a "vagrant-free zone" in which homeless persons would be subject to arrest.

The Central Area Study was commissioned in connection with the development of Underground Atlanta, a $142 million dollar project aimed at revitalizing a shopping and entertainment core of the city. The project itself would conveniently eliminate Plaza Park and thus remove one place of refuge for the homeless. The homeless must go since they might frighten away conventioneers and suburban shoppers. The development of Underground Atlanta had been a priority of Mayor Andrew

PHOTOGRAPHS © DIETRICK GERSTNER

"WOLF" THOMAS (ABOVE) AND THE VAGRANT CHRIST, 1986

Young since his election in 1982. Its financing was an intricate web of city and federal monies and private investment. After many legal challenges, construction began in 1987.

The Open Door Community responded to the development of Underground Atlanta and what it represented for the homeless by mounting a long campaign that had essentially two goals. First, the Open Door wanted the city to replace Plaza Park with another park where homeless persons would not be hassled. The community suggested that the park be named in honor of Al Smith, a homeless man who had been killed at a shelter. Second, the community wanted to keep people aware of the situation of the homeless and how money spent on Underground Atlanta should have gone to housing. In fact, the project involved $8 million from Community Development Block Grant funds intended for housing and jobs for the poor.

Another $12 million came from a city sales tax which the Open Door saw as money that should have been used to address the needs of the city's poor.

In addition to numerous meetings with city officials concerning the Al Smith Park, the community began weekly picketing and leafleting in Woodruff Park. In April 1987, Open Door Community members tied crosses to the construction fence surrounding Plaza Park. Each cross represented a person who had died on the streets of Atlanta from exposure and neglect. One day a week throughout the summer of 1987, the community marched from Woodruff Park, down Peachtree past the Underground Atlanta construction site, to the steps of City Hall. Along the way, community members sang, beat old soup pots, and leafleted. They hoped to keep alive the issue of how the plans for a revitalized downtown were based on the exclusion of the poor and homeless. The reception of the community's actions by downtown shoppers and business people eating lunch in Woodruff Park was often hostile. The community in its actions and leaflets sought to represent a view of Atlanta from the underside where those who had lost in the competitive marketplace languished.

By the time Underground Atlanta opened on June 15, 1989, little had changed in the city with regard to the homeless. The Open Door Community led a protest in which they were joined by supporters from Atlanta Advocates for the Homeless, Jubilee Partners, and Koinonia Farm. Picketing and leafleting took place at the entrances to Underground to remind people heading into the shopping and entertainment complex: "In this same year that Atlanta has spent $142 million to develop Underground as entertainment for the well-to-do, 40,000 men, women, and children have slept in shelters for the homeless. LET'S GET OUR PRIORITIES STRAIGHT!!!!!!" The reverse side of the leaflet noted that the financing for the development of Underground had been taken from government funds intended for housing and jobs for the poor. The leaflet concluded, "We see nothing inherently wrong with the development of entertainment facilities. But when the overwhelming resources of the city go into entertainment while the suffering of the poor is largely ignored or dismissed, we are building a broken community."

Inside of Underground Atlanta when Mayor Young began his speech to laud its opening, six protesters (Ed Loring, Elizabeth Dede, Ty Brown, Tim Wyse, and Pete Stinner from the Open Door, and Steve Clemens from Koinonia) sounded air horns and chanted "Atlanta keeps the homeless underground." They were quickly arrested. Elizabeth recalls that when she was brought up to the cellblock wearing the fashionable clothes needed to enter the Underground Atlanta celebration, one of the women said to her, "What are you in for? Staying in church too long?" Sharing in their laughter, Elizabeth was taken under their wing as they made sure she got a mat and a blanket.

Mayor Young, visibly upset by the protest, nervously claimed that Atlanta was committed to addressing the needs of the homeless. His actions as mayor, however, belied his words. Mayor Young's attitude was that the city had little responsibility for the homeless. It was a problem best left with Atlanta's churches. He thought the most the city government could do was to encourage investment which would supposedly lead to jobs. Underground Atlanta represented for him the best possible response to homelessness since it combined white business interests with African-American political power. In his view, such development would provide both jobs and a vibrant downtown gathering place.

During the Fall of 1993 the community took on one more aspect of the ongoing attempt to enforce a "Vagrant-Free Zone." One of the laws made it illegal to lie down on a park bench. On September 13, eleven members of the Open Door and "People for Urban Justice" went to Woodruff Park to challenge the ordinance. They lay down on park benches and refused to move when instructed to do so by police officers. They were arrested and spent 24 hours in jail and were then sentenced to "time served." Elizabeth remembers that the time in jail was one more place of connection and joy with the poor who were being harassed by the "Vagrant-Free Zone" laws:

> Since most everyone in the jail was poor and African American, they were really curious to know what these middle-class white women were doing there. When Gladys told them she had been picked up for prostitution, they roared with laughter. In response, Gladys did a little provocative dance and asked, "Don't you think I've got what it takes?" The jail was filled with giggles and belly laughs and shouts: "Mama's in for prostitution."

On October 4, ten more people were arrested for again violating the ordinance. They were sentenced to one day in the City Prison Farm or a fine of $58. On October 18, the City Council, responding to a call from Council President Marvin Arrington to remove the law, voted unanimously to do so.

Toward the end of his term, Mayor Young worked to promote the selection of Atlanta for the 1996 Olympic Games, promising the city an economic windfall from the selection. As with Underground Atlanta, Mayor Young did not seek to insure that the economic benefits of the Olympic Games would in fact reach the poor of the city, or that the monies would be used to develop low-income housing. In fact, the Olympic Village housing, built on space where public housing was torn down, was turned over to Georgia Tech for student dormitories after the Games. Throughout the build-up to the Olympic Games the Open Door protested, raising the issue of the enormous amount of money—public and private—being spent on the Games while the poor were displaced from their homes and neighborhoods, and the harassment and imprisonment of the homeless worsened. By 1995 the National Law Center on Homelessness and Poverty identified Atlanta as one of five cities in the U.S. with the "meanest streets." Atlanta's policies of restrictions on uses of public spaces and begging, selective enforcement of laws, and "sweeps" of homeless people from the streets before major conventions or other events earned the city this designation. The Open Door in its protests confronted the "city too busy to hate" as a city that organized hatred against the homeless.

THE CAMPAIGN FOR AFFORDABLE HOUSING AND THE TAKEOVER OF THE IMPERIAL HOTEL, 1990–1996

In the spring of 1990, a new wave of police harassment and arrests of homeless persons took place. Members of the Open Door Community, out on the streets for their annual Holy Week with the Homeless, were told by a policeman they could not sleep on the steps of the Fulton County Health Department across the street from Grady Hospital. His reason: "Lots of big people drive along this street, and they don't want to see you. You've got to get up and move on." The vagrant-free zone had apparently been put into effect. Homeless advocates, including the Open Door, saw the city administration continuing to accept the myth: "Whatever benefits the central business district benefits everyone."

The Imperial Hotel once had been a single resident occupancy hotel that provided low cost housing for the poor. Soon after its purchase by John Portman, a very influential and wealthy developer in Atlanta, the hotel was closed. It was an apt symbol for the city's and the business community's unwillingness to address the shortage of housing in the city for the poor and homeless. Standing on the corner of Peachtree Street and

IMPERIAL HOTEL, 1990

Ralph McGill Boulevard in downtown Atlanta, the eight-story building, constructed in 1910, sat empty for ten years, slowly deteriorating from neglect.

On a warm June morning in 1990, eight people from "People for Urban Justice" entered the abandoned Imperial Hotel: Murphy Davis, Elizabeth Dede, Sister Carol Schlicksup, C. M. Sherman, Larry Travick, Ed Loring, John Flournoy, and Sister Jo Ann Geary. Of these eight, seven were members of the Open Door Community. The Open Door intended the takeover of the Imperial Hotel to be a dramatic statement of the need for affordable housing in Atlanta and the availability of resources to provide that housing. Those who occupied the building pointed to the city's actions over the past several years in which money that could have gone toward housing was instead earmarked for commercial development. Especially galling was the diversion of $8 million dollars from the Federal government—intended for low-income housing and jobs—but used to help develop Underground Atlanta. But the protestors also pointed to the city's wooing of the Super Bowl and plan to build a new indoor football stadium, along with the 1996 Summer Olympics. Both of these were evidence that money could be found for high profile entertainment events, while little was offered to address the needs of the poor and homeless in the city.

Shortly after occupying the building, the protestors unfurled a banner from the top floor of the hotel which said, "House the Homeless Here." Through a megaphone, Ed Loring and Murphy Davis called out to people on the streets below to join in the protest, and to ask Mayor Maynard Jackson and John Portman to join them in building housing for the homeless. On the sidewalks, other members of the Open Door and friends of the community picketed with signs asking how money could be found for Underground Atlanta, a new domed stadium, and the Olympics, while none was available for housing. In a letter sent to Portman, the protestors stated that they had "re-opened the building to show you, and Joe Martin of Central Atlanta Progress, and Mayor Jackson the way to provide single room occupancy housing."

As morning passed into afternoon, word spread on the streets about the takeover of the hotel. Homeless men, women, and children soon appeared asking those inside if they could come in and stay. A welcome was extended and the hotel began to fill up with people in need of shelter. The protestors had assumed that the police would arrest them before noon. By early evening they and the almost seventy homeless people who had joined them were still there. Portman, possibly fearing a public relations nightmare, did not sign the necessary police complaint to have them removed.

As people moved in, they were asked to help clean up whatever room they would occupy. On Tuesday, a pile of debris began to appear on the sidewalk and street outside the hotel as homeless persons worked tirelessly to turn the building into a home. By Wednesday morning, the pile was large enough to block the street in front of the hotel. City officials demanded that Portman Properties remove the debris since it came from the hotel they owned. At 11:00 A.M., the company gave in to city pressures and sent a bulldozer to clean up the streets. A large dumpster was then placed in the street to contain the debris being hauled out by the homeless renovators of the hotel.

Upon his return to town the day after the takeover, Mayor Jackson met with Portman. He persuaded Portman not to evict the people from the hotel, and then went to the Imperial and urged the people there to be cooperative. He told them they would be allowed to stay until July 2. On Wednesday after a tour of the hotel, Jackson encouraged the protesters and squatters to leave, saying the building was unsafe and the city would open a temporary shelter for the homeless at Grady High School. Few from the hotel accepted the offer. One of them, Bill Jones, told the mayor, "We don't want your shelter. We want housing."

By this time, the Open Door had moved most of its daily operations to the Imperial. Members of the community were sleeping at the hotel; meals were being served; and a portable generator had been set up to provide light inside the building. Community members were also assisting in the organization of the homeless people who had taken up residence so that they could live peacefully and safely in the hotel. Leadership emerged from within this homeless community. They were finding a power and voice which had long eluded them. They were not going to be easily budged from the hotel by promises from politicians or business leaders. Laura Cooper was one of these leaders from among the homeless. She explained their position in simple forceful language to a local newspaper: "This is our house. That's how we see it. We're just asking them [city leaders] to let us do this for ourselves. Is that wrong?"

While the occupation continued into its second week, Nelson Mandela the great leader of South Africans' drive for liberation from apartheid came to Atlanta as part of his tour of the United States. Much as they wanted to hear Mandela speak at nearby Georgia Tech, the squatters refused to leave, fearing the city would not allow them back into the building. Meanwhile, negotiations continued between homeless leaders in the hotel, city officials, and representatives from Portman Properties. On July 3 the mayor signed an agreement whereby the city promised to build 3,500 units of single room occupancy housing over the next three and half years, and also to open "Welcome House," a shelter on Memorial Drive which the homeless themselves would control. Bill Jones, one of the leaders among the homeless, said the takeover had forced the city to take notice of homelessness, and that it had accomplished more in two weeks "than committees have done in seven years." Most of the homeless left the Imperial for the Memorial Drive shelter after this agreement. Some returned to the streets.

Still, not all of the people who occupied the building were happy with the agreement. Some believed it had been reached only under the threat of arrest for criminal trespass. Further, it was not providing housing now, but only more shelter space. Finally, they still sought a meeting with John Portman to discuss the needs of the homeless and to urge him to provide resources to develop housing for the poor. For these reasons, six of the original protestors refused to leave the hotel as demanded by Mayor Jackson and Portman Properties. On July 3, Ed Loring, Murphy Davis, Carol Schlicksup, JoAnn Geary, Elizabeth Dede, and John Flournoy were removed from the hotel and arrested. The takeover had ended.

The occupation of the Imperial Hotel, initiated by the Open Door, had taken on a life of its own. When it ended, the community knew that they had been part of something much larger than they had anticipated or planned. The city and the business community had been startled into some action. Homeless persons had stood up to the powers with some success. A sense of their own strength in organizing themselves and confronting city and business leaders had taken root and grown. The plight of homeless persons in the city had received broad coverage in newspapers and on television. Many people had seen how eager homeless persons were to work to create a place they could call home. Six years after the takeover, in 1996, the Imperial Hotel re-opened as a 120 unit low-income, residential living facility. An organization called Progressive Redevelopment, Inc., which had entered into negotiations with the city on the heels of the takeover, advocates from the Open Door and other organizations continued with public pressure, and funding from a variety of sources was finally acquired for the renovation.

THE GRADY CAMPAIGN FOR HEALTH CARE, 1999—PRESENT

Many of the stories in the Gospels show Jesus engaged in the work of healing. Jesus heals persons marginalized for being sick. Jesus responds to their need with compassion and the power to heal. Given the poverty in the land in which Jesus lived, it is no surprise that he encountered many sick and troubled people, and he encountered resistance to his practice of free medical care. In Jesus' day, as today, being poor means not having enough of the necessities of life, and being poor increases the likelihood of developing sicknesses and then not having enough to pay for medical care.

Grady Hospital is Atlanta's only public hospital and the state's most important teaching hospital and trauma center.

© CALVIN KIMBROUGH

GRADY HOSPITAL BOARD MEETING, 1999

Grady trains physicians from the Emory University and Morehouse College medical schools. Like other public hospitals in the United States, it has seen a dramatic increase in the number of uninsured patients as people increasingly cannot afford to pay for medical insurance and/or companies do not provide such coverage for their workers. At the same time, Grady has seen reductions in federal, state, and local government financial support. These factors combined to create huge deficits in the hospital's budget, and as a result a variety of cuts and increases to charges for patients were proposed by the Grady Board to the Fulton and DeKalb County commissioners, the two government entities that provide the bulk of public funding for Grady.

Beginning in 1992 the DeKalb and Fulton County Commissions steadily cut their financial support for Grady. The state of Georgia at the same time was reducing its funding, while federal dollars were also reduced some $28 million due to two pieces of federal legislation, the Welfare Reform Act of 1996 and the Balanced Budget Act of 1997. The former had resulted in fewer Medicare dollars going to Grady, as people who had gone "from welfare to work" ended up in low-paying jobs without medical insurance and with their access to Medicare denied. Without Medicare they still relied, however, on Grady for medical care. Only now Medicare would not be reimbursing Grady for that care.

As 1999 began, Grady faced a $26.4 million deficit. To make some dent in that deficit, the Grady administration announced in February that beginning March 15, 1999, the hospital would begin charging its poorest patients $5 for each clinic visit and a minimum $10 co-payment for each prescription and any additional medical supplies. Further, the Grady Board approved, but did not publicize, that $4.9 million would still be set aside to provide assistance to those without money. From the standpoint of the Grady Board, the costs passed on to the poor were reasonably small financial requirements.

The approximately 25,000 poor people affected by the policy saw things differently. They quickly experienced how the policy affected their access to medical care. As the policy went into effect, many of the poor who depended upon Grady for medications found themselves having to choose between prescriptions because they could not afford the $10 co-pay on each prescription. Some of these ended up being hospitalized as the lack of prescriptions compounded their medical conditions. Murphy Davis and Elizabeth Dede, writing in the April 1999 issue of *Hospitality,* noted that at least one death appeared related to the new policy. In the May *Hospitality,* Dr. Neil Shulman, a physician at Grady and a professor of medicine at Emory University Medical School, stated that doctors in the emergency room at Grady "reported visits of patients with heart failure, with recurrent bouts of pancreatitis and many other ailments because they were not able to afford their medications."

In the early spring of 1999, the Coalition for Grady Patients/Friends of Grady Hospital was formed. It sought to pressure Grady to end this policy and to work to ensure that

Grady would receive the funding necessary to continue its services to the poor. The Coalition represented a broad group of people who were either directly harmed by the policy or saw the harm it was causing as a grave injustice. Members included the Open Door Community, People for Urban Justice, Concerned Black Clergy, Southern Prison Ministry, Fulton-Atlanta Community Action Authority, the AIDS Survival Project, Rainbow/Push Coalition, ACT-UP/Atlanta, Southern Christian Leadership Conference, Oakhurst Presbyterian Church, a variety of labor unions, and individual professors and students from Emory University School of Medicine, along with doctors, staff, and patients of Grady Hospital. Coalition members began to gather information about adverse affects of the policy on people seeking prescriptions and other services at Grady. They also began informational pickets at the hospital.

On March 15, Coalition members gained a meeting with Mr. Edward Renford, the President and CEO of Grady Health System. They had entered the hospital demanding to meet with him, and after nearly two hours of singing, chanting, and refusing to leave, a meeting was arranged. It lasted over five hours. Though no changes were forthcoming, the Coalition members learned at this point of the $4.9 million set aside to provide assistance to those without money for prescriptions and clinic visits.

On March 22, about fifty members of the Coalition attended a Grady Board meeting to urge that the policy changes adversely affecting the poor be ended. Various members of the Coalition testified to the ill effects the changes were having on the poor. The Board eventually approved a motion to reduce the co-pay to 50 cents. The Coalition pledged to seek additional funding for Grady from Atlanta, Fulton, and DeKalb counties, the state and federal governments, and private sources.

On April 7, some 200 advocates from the Coalition urged

the Fulton County Commission to increase funding for Grady. The County Commissioners voted to find another $3.5 million for the Grady pharmacy. A few days later on April 13, advocates gathered at a meeting of the DeKalb County Commission seeking $1.1 million to address the Grady needs. Police were called in to remove those urging the Commission to approve this request for additional monies. Seven people were arrested. Reflecting an inability to understand the need for significant public dollars to address the crisis and/or mean-spiritedness, the CEO of the DeKalb County Commission, Liane Levetan, proposed that churches and synagogues take up a collection for Grady.

When the County Commission met on May 11, Coalition members again urged additional funds for Grady. This time thirty advocates were arrested as the Commission again refused to allocate money for the hospital. Those arrested included doctors, patients, labor leaders, and clergy, among them the Rev. Tim McDonald of Concerned Black Clergy. In the June meeting of the County Commission, the $1.1 million was approved with country commissioners stating that they had not been influenced in their voting by the demonstrations. At the state level the Coalition organized a July "March for Medicine," and by September Governor Roy Barnes announced a plan that eventually led to $53 million in funding for Grady.

Meanwhile the Coalition was also stepping up pressure upon the private medical schools that used Grady Hospital for teaching and research. The Coalition urged Emory University to comply with a 1984 contract requiring Emory to provide support and full medical staffing to Grady Hospital. Emory's medical school had used Grady for years as a research and teaching hospital. But Emory had in the early 1990s formed a partnership with Columbia/HCA, a for-profit health care corporation. In the years that followed, Emory began to reduce its commitment to Grady and increase the number of doctors and medical students at its own private hospital, Crawford-Long. In doing this, Emory was following a national trend in medical schools. Several Emory doctors joined with the Grady Coalition and protested Emory's financial and medical staff reductions in relation to Grady. One, Dr. Sam Newcom, a physician for over 35 years, was placed on administrative leave by Emory University for his participation and threatened with the loss of his faculty position.

The Coalition has continued to pressure Grady and local government to continue care for the poor and uninsured. The Coalition has met with some success. It was able to stop the policy of charging the poorest of the poor $10 for each prescription and $5 for clinic visits. It was able to pressure Fulton and DeKalb county governments and the state to give monies to pull Grady through its immediate financial crisis. It was able to advocate for changes that led to improvements in the Grady pharmacy system. And, as part of its success, it continues to be a multi-racial, multi-class coalition that monitors funding for Grady and agitates when necessary to insure continued care for the poor who are served by the hospital.

THE "LET'S DO DOWNTOWN" CAMPAIGN, 2003

In the winter of 2003, Mayor Shirley Franklin appointed a commission to do yet another study of the problem of homelessness in Atlanta. She appointed lawyers, bankers, and a municipal court judge who was well known by homeless people for his severe sentences for their violation of "quality of life" ordinances. Conspicuously absent from the commission were homeless people and representatives from groups who had an adversarial relationship with city government on issues having to do with homelessness, such as the Open Door. At the same time, the city and business leaders were going ahead with fund-raising for a $200 million aquarium to attract more tourists downtown and discussing raising $300 million in private funds for a new symphony hall, while Grady Hospital was facing a $20 million deficit.

By the spring of 2003 the study was complete, and the commission issued its "Blueprint to End Homelessness in Atlanta." Among the Mayor's actions to implement the "Blueprint" the first was a 100-day period for the summer months called "Let's Do Downtown" that would feature music and other events in Woodruff Park, along with a substantial increase in police action against homeless people. During that time the Mayor, Central Atlanta Progress, and the Atlanta Downtown Neighborhood Association joined together to urge that serving people meals in the park be ended. Mayor Franklin issued an executive order banning meals in the park. Additionally, police were instructed to arrest persons lying down on park benches or the grass.

Woodruff Park, as it had been so many times before, again became contested space. The Open Door joined with other groups to resist the "cleansing." The resistance took a variety of forms. When the city offered an "open mic" on Fridays for poetry, community members signed up and read poems denouncing the Mayor's policies. Eventually the city stopped the open-mic event. Community members would stay in the park and observe police action. If police attempted to make a homeless person not lay on a bench, community members would lie down on benches. While doing so, they would point out that there was no law against lying down on a bench, thanks to the Open Door's actions in 1993.

Some police officers themselves contacted the Open Door and organized a morning event in which community members lay down in a park where the police had been told to do "sweep" of homeless persons. The police arrived and called their superiors telling them that persons were refusing to move. Eventually those in command had to admit there was no legal basis for telling people in the park to get up and leave. Also, in defiance of the Mayor's executive order, groups continued to feed homeless persons in the park. The Mayor declined to have anyone arrested in the park, though one minister was arrested while feeding people on a street near a city shelter. His charge was a parking violation. Chuck Harris and Diana George, both resident volunteers, wrote of the resistance efforts in the context of the Open Door's commitment to a vision of life contrary to that urged by the business and political elite:

> Making a better world means rejecting the idea of prosperity through wealth and nonstop entertainment, with lots of police and military to keep us "safe." Making a better world means taking some responsibility for the way homeless people are treated. And, for Christians, if we take discipleship seriously, making a better world ought to mean raising a voice of outrage.

A TRADITION OF PROPHETIC POLITICS

In "raising a voice of outrage" the Open Door Community's actions over the years may be understood as prophetic politics. Such politics follow the tradition of the Hebrew prophets, Jesus, and many other nonviolent resisters over the centuries. Prophetic politics engages in public symbolic acts to dramatize faith convictions that criticize dominant cultural values and practices. In these actions, the protesters seek to shed light upon injustices ignored or hidden and thus call people to recognize a shared responsibility for changing the injustices.

When the Open Door uses biblical words to call for justice for the poor, the homeless, and the imprisoned, it asserts the public power of God's word. Religious convictions and biblical themes have often informed political life in the South. Biblical language and imagery have a particular resonance in the Bible

Belt. Still, the power of the Bible has often been restricted by a prevalent moralism in most churches that is concerned only with private life and an otherworldly salvation. The Open Door's prophetic politics recalls the wholistic thrust of the biblical call which insists that the reign of God enter into and transform all areas of life.

The energy and motivation for the prophetic politics of the Open Door is tied into the community's work of hospitality. In reflecting upon their own existence as a community and their work, members of the Open Door see the faith convictions and political implications expressed in their daily tasks, and so they see the need to act more explicitly to urge a biblical vision of justice. A community handbook from the mid-1980s stated:

> The soup kitchen is also a sign of the degradation, violence, and injustice with which this nation is filled. Hunger is a political manifestation of an economic system which serves the rich and starves the poor. We must never be satisfied with feeding the hungry Christ. Our compassion for the poor must be channeled into analysis and action that struggles to change the political and economic systems which are the root of hunger in America.

The community's faith commitment to Christ, enacted in their life with the poor, also necessitates political involvement for justice. This is yet another manifestation of the wholeness of the community's faith which places all of life under God and so refuses to separate charity from justice, faith from social action. Public protest and advocacy on behalf of the homeless and imprisoned is necessary if the community is to be faithful to the Jesus who proclaimed and enacted the reign of God. Murphy writes:

> Our little crumbs of service are not enough. What

> the poor and downtrodden need is not our piecemeal charity but justice. Not that we will close the soup kitchen or shower line or shelters. Not that we will stop visiting in the prisons and jails or stop writing letters. But this is not an answer. An answer would only come in the form of justice. Wholeness. Enough for all God's children. . . . We must find the way to embody/incarnate the misery of the poor in the public arena.

The political vision and practices of the community thus do not reflect those of classical liberalism which aims toward compromise and the balancing of the interests of the powerful. Instead, the community seeks to question this whole approach of interest-based politics that has little or no conception of a common good and even less concern for the well-being of society's most vulnerable members. This chapter has focused on the community's prophetic politics in challenging the dominant political and business responses to homelessness in Atlanta. In the next chapter, the community's political action on behalf of the imprisoned and those threatened by the death penalty will be detailed.

In their prophetic actions that dramatize the injustices done to the homeless the Open Door continues to challenge the political and business elite myth: "Whatever benefits the central business district benefits everyone." The mixed results of the community's actions to date point to the ongoing power this myth has for those who run the institutions of government and business in the city of Atlanta. But these results also give witness to the tenacity of the Open Door Community and its faith that God is opposed to the injustice and exploitation found in this city. In its resistance on the streets of Atlanta, the community continues to offer an alternative vision, the vision of the Beloved Community in which all fully participate with human dignity in forming a good life together.

10

FAITHFUL RESISTANCE TO IMPRISONMENT AND THE DEATH PENALTY

MURPHY DAVIS RELATES THAT ROBERT PENN WARREN was asked once about what ought to be done in response to the many problems facing American society. He responded, "Well, I think the first thing we ought to do is to stop lying to each other." Just as truth-telling is needed to counter the lie that whatever benefits the central business district benefits everyone, so too, truth telling is needed when the U.S. imprisons a larger proportion of people than any other nation in history, when 45 million people are without medical insurance, and when our rates of violence, infant mortality, and child poverty are higher than any other Western democracy, while at the same time a political and economic elite continues to amass great wealth. The faithful resistance by the Open Door in relation to prisons and the death penalty has been one of truth-telling through articles in *Hospitality*, public speaking and education, campaigns that have brought needed change for those in prison, vigils at the time of executions, and other acts of witness.

One important work of the community is informing people about the realities of prison life. A favorite political strategy by those who want to increase the number of those behind bars and to justify inhumane treatment of the imprisoned is to lie about how easy it is to be behind bars in the United States. The lies of "country club prisons" and "luxurious imprisonment" are used to justify treatment that further dehumanizes those in our nation's jails and prisons. These lies have resulted in the almost complete dismantling of rehabilitation programs in jails and prisons and the creation of "super max" prisons that are among the most inhumane and torturous in human history.

Hospitality frequently publishes articles and letters from people in prison who describe a very different reality than the lies about an easy life behind bars. In a February 2000 *Hospitality* article titled "The Soul Stealers," a prisoner who has been a friend of the Open Door Community since its beginning described prison life:

> What transpires when a person is sent to one of our nation's ever-burgeoning prisons? One would think that our prison system would educate and train the prisoner to be a law-abiding, productive member of our society. But this is far from what is accomplished. What happens is that the person who enters prison is emotionally, psychologically, spiritually and sometimes

> physically attacked. You are humiliated and dehumanized. Everything is taken from you—your dignity, your thought processes, even your sense of right and wrong is undermined. . . . Nothing beneficial to you comes easy in prison. . . . Countless thousands of men and women come to prison guilty of making a few bad choices in life. After years, if not decades, of mentally and morally crushing treatment by prison officials, they leave filled with a bitter hatred towards society. . . . Because hatred is fostered by the prison administration, the system effectively causes countless thousands to lose their souls. For with a heart filled with hatred, the Christian lives in sin. For those who call themselves religious people, these [prison] agencies are effectively stealing souls in your name. What excuse will you give when on that day of judgment you confront your Creator who then asks why you did nothing (or so little) while so many souls were being stolen?

The Open Door seeks in its truth-telling about prisons and the death penalty to help those in prison resist having their souls stolen through brutal torturous treatment and inhumane conditions.

Similarly, the community continually points out the gap between the right wing promotion of a perception of crime run wild that leads to more and more imprisonment, and the reality that a "lock 'em up" response to crime does not create a safer and more secure society. Nibs Stroupe, a longtime friend of the community, wrote in *Hospitality:*

> One would think that in a country that locks up so many of its people, we would feel safe and secure. We do not. We feel insecure and anxious. We believe that our criminal justice system is soft on crime, that those

> serving time in our prisons and jails are being coddled. One wonders what it will take in this country to make us feel safe.

Consistent with an Open Door analysis of American society, Nibs identified two reasons for our ongoing insecurity, a materialistic consumerism and racism:

> While a sense of security is fundamental to life as a human being, our culture has made it impossible for us to feel secure. Our economy is driven by creating a desire in us for things to make us feel secure, then offering a better "thing" to make us feel more secure. Yet, what is the result? We never feel secure. Why? As long as we feel good because we have things, we will have an immense insecurity. . . . We can't feel good if someone can take our goods.

In terms of racism, Nibs notes the fear of black males and how keeping large numbers of black males in prison is reassuring to the white majority. The beginning of the "get tough on crime," and thus the initiating of the rise in imprisonment in the United States, coincided with the year 1968. Nibs observes:

> The reason for the massive build-up in prisons in this country is . . . white fear of freedom movements among people of darker color. We do not seriously consider alternatives to incarceration because we want black males locked up and out of our presence. . . . The current purpose of this system is to make us feel secure, and we feel most secure when as many black males as possible are locked up.

Nibs recognizes that many would consider this analysis

far-fetched or ridiculous. But, along with the Open Door Community, he points to the numbers. In 1970, white people made up 60.5 percent of the prison population, while people of color made up 39.55. In 2003, the percentage of black men in prison is approximately double that of white men. Per capita blacks are nine times more likely than whites to have been in jail. A visit to the Atlanta City Detention Center, or to almost any major city's jail, corroborates these statistics.

The Open Door recognizes and tells the truth. The jails and prisons in this nation reflect the nation's racism and dysfunctional economic system. Murphy reflected upon the execution of Chris Burger in 1993 to point to the deadly consequences of vengeful political rhetoric and public policies that have led to an explosion in the rate of imprisonment and continuing endorsement of executions:

> It would be safe to say that the state of Georgia spent some three to five million on the process of disposing of Chris Burger. Through his early childhood of abuse and neglect, there were never any resources for Chris. But when the time came that he finally stepped over the line, the most enormous resources imaginable were marshalled to get rid of him. We have heard and tolerated a language of hatred and alienation for so long that we have begun to believe that we are powerless to call on the forces of goodness and kindness among us. We are afraid of our children, and our minds, spirits, and imaginations have been paralyzed by the fear.

The fear powers the ongoing building of prisons, the mistreatment of prisoners, and the death penalty. The Open Door offers the truth of which Jesus spoke, "You shall know the truth and it will set you free" (John 8:32).

HARDWICK TEACHING TRIP

We saw in chapter seven that as part of the Hardwick Trip, in which the community provides transportation for family members of those imprisoned at Hardwick Prison in Milledgeville, Murphy will occasionally do a "teaching trip." While family members are visiting their loved ones in prison, Murphy gives a "truth-telling" tour of the prison grounds to those who volunteer to drive or come on the trip. On this tour, she explains that the complex of buildings that constitutes the Hardwick Prison is actually a large campus that was once the state mental hospital.

The hospital began in 1842 as the Georgia Lunatic Asylum. Slave labor was used to run the hospital. After the war, the hospital began to employ local people and it grew rapidly. Its name changes over the year reveal changes in views of mental illness. In the late 1800s it became a "sanitarium," then in the 1920s it became a "hospital." For many years people were committed to the hospital for illnesses that were poorly understood, if at all. Women were sometimes put away when husbands wanted to be freed to marry another. Like the story in Mark's Gospel where people see Jesus as "being out of his mind" because of his association with disreputable people, Clarence Jordan, who founded the interracial Koinonia Farm, was almost put away by his family who were embarrassed by his associating with blacks and his work for justice.

Deinstitutionalization in the 1970s emptied out most of the wards of the hospital. When the federal and state governments failed to create promised half-way houses and treatment centers, many of those released ended up on the streets. At the same time, local politicians worked hard to ensure that the buildings left empty would find a use that would help the economy of Baldwin County where the hospital was located. In 1980, the "Rivers Buildings" were re-opened as prisons.

© CALVIN KIMBROUGH

HARDWICK TEACHING TRIP, 2005

Over the next twenty years, most of the other buildings also re-opened as prisons as the state prison population surged to nearly 50,000 people.

Some of the former mental hospital patients who ended up on the streets now frequent the Open Door. George, who spends much of his time in the front yard of the Open Door, was once an "inmate" at Milledgeville. Some of those patients have also ended up back at Hardwick, imprisoned rather than being treated for their mental illness. Conditions in the prison have garnered attention over the years as abuse of prisoners has taken place. The physical set-up itself is brutalizing. In the Rivers Building, there are six huge dormitories with 75 double-bunked cots located just a few feet apart. The lights never go off. The dorm is never completely quiet. Personal space is non-existent. Under such conditions, being able to get out of the dorm for a visit is truly a blessing.

The teaching trip ends at one of the six cemeteries on the grounds in which some 30,000 people are buried. The cemeteries were once segregated by race and gender. Most of the graves are now unmarked. When power mowers were introduced in the 1960s, workers pulled up and tossed aside the simple metal markers on each grave. Murphy closes by talking about how nature "has healed in some ways, brought some healing beauty to a place where people were just thrown away, forgotten, buried. But the cemeteries remain as a symbol of what we tend to do with each other: give up, and throw away."

GEORGIA WOMEN'S PRISON SCANDAL

In visiting prisoners and in providing transportation for family members of those in prison, the Open Door learns of conditions inside of the prisons. Thus, the Open Door has come to learn firsthand that in addition to racism and classism, the evil of sexism permeates the criminal justice system.

According to Amnesty International, there are estimated to be more than 80,000 mothers among the women in U.S. prisons and jails. They have approximately 200,000 children under 18. All states have laws permitting the termination of parental rights of parents who are incarcerated. In 1997–98, more than 2,200 pregnant women were imprisoned and more than 1,300 babies were born to women in prison. In at least 40 states, babies are taken from their imprisoned mothers almost immediately after birth or at the time the mother is discharged from the hospital. Since 1980, the number of female inmates in U.S. prisons has increased more than 500 percent.

In Georgia, a woman's likelihood of going to prison is two times the national average. Georgia's female prison population more than doubled from 1989 to 1999. In August 1999, Georgia's female inmate population of 2,474 was ranked 6th highest in the nation. Women in Georgia state prisons were overwhelmingly mothers: 54 percent had 1–2 children; 41 percent had 3–5 children; 4 percent had more than five children. Of the women in state prisons, 44 percent reported that they were physically or sexually assaulted at some time during their lives. Among the women, a high percentage were deemed mentally ill. In Georgia's inmate population, 28 percent of females were classified as mentally ill versus 10.8 percent of males. A total of 24 percent of female inmates in state prisons in 1998 were identified as mentally ill.

In 1984, a class action lawsuit was filed by both men and women imprisoned at Hardwick, officially known as the Middle Georgia Correctional Complex. This lawsuit, *Cason v. Seckinger,* sought injunctive relief to remedy numerous alleged constitutional violations related to conditions of confinement. In the early 1990s the story broke of systemic abuse of women prisoners at Hardwick. It was reported that guards and other prison staff regularly practiced sexual and physical abuse against many women in the prison. Nearly 200 women made accusations of abuse implicating some 50 staff members.

The abuses alleged included rape, the offering of special favors and favorable parole recommendations in exchange for sex, the punishment of some women who refused sexual contact, mental health "treatment" that included stripping, hog-tying, chaining and isolating mentally ill and suicidal prisoners, drug and prostitution rings operated by the prison staff, and placing women in physical restraints and seclusion for days at a time, during which they were often stripped naked and observed on camera by male officers. In many cases the women had made reports about the abuse but nothing was done. One woman claimed that she had been impregnated by a staff member and was forced to have an abortion. Women also alleged that their complaints about the abuse went unheeded and were never investigated. Women complained that they suffered emotional and psychological harm, but did not receive appropriate counseling to deal with the trauma. Murphy wrote:

> A similar but quieter scandal occurred in the women's

> prison some 10 years ago when five men were fired or "allowed to retire" for sexually violating women. The Department of Corrections rearranged things a bit and went on. Obviously the problem was not addressed. We need to understand when an institution exists in which men hold keys and power and women are completely without power, there will be abuse. A women's prison is simply an exaggerated expression of our society and its values. Sexism is violent and deadly and cannot be addressed by firing some "bad" guards and hiring a fresh batch. The system must be overhauled and must include stringent safeguards that guarantee the safety and dignity of women prisoners.

To bring public pressure to bear in relation to the lawsuit and the stories of abuse that emerged, Murphy in her role as the director of the Southern Prison Ministry acted along with other organizations to help form the "Coalition for Justice for Women in Prison." The Coalition included such groups as Amnesty International, the Southern Christian Leadership Conference, the ACLU, Atlanta Clergy and Laity Concerned, and Concerned Black Clergy. They organized to publicize the charges and pressure the state government to respond vigorously to correct the abuses.

Part of the pressure included public demonstrations, such as on December 11, 1992, when 100 people gathered for a demonstration outside of the Georgia Women's Prison at Hardwick. A prisoner wrote of the demonstration, "The vigil was wonderful. The women in here are not used to having people stand up for them. No, quite the opposite; they are used to betrayal and lies. No amount of words on earth could have meant as much as the tangible show of concern and belief in us did." The story began to get national attention as the ABC News Program "Day One" and the *Oprah Winfrey Show* aired reports on the abuse.

As a result of the litigation, the state indicted 17 staff members for sexual abuse of women inmates. Of those indicted only one lieutenant was brought to trial with 20 women ready to testify against him. The trial took place in Baldwin county where the prison was located; a county that benefited financially from the many prisons located there. The lieutenant was acquitted. Six of those indicted pled guilty to the offenses. A few others were demoted, fired, suspended, transferred or quit. The state also entered a series of consent decrees from 1992 to 1995 that (1) allowed women to report misconduct confidentially and protected them from retaliation; (2) provided for counseling to women who had experienced sexual abuse by staff members; (3) established protocols for the use of physical restraints and seclusion for mentally ill women; (4) prohibited the stripping of women except in very limited circumstances; (5) established procedures for investigation of sexual contact, sexual harassment, and sexual abuse of women inmates; and (6) established training of employees and female inmates about sexual abuse, sexual contact, and sexual harassment. The court entered an order on March 7, 1994, that permanently enjoined sexual contact, sexual harassment, and sexual abuse of women inmates by staff. The women's prison was also relocated from Milledgeville to Atlanta.

The fallout from the abuse scandal continued into 1993. On April 1, 1993, Governor Zell Miller transferred Department of Corrections Commissioner Bobby Whitworth to the Board of Pardons and Parole. Murphy commented that "regrettably the governor's actions seemed more to be responses to a public relations problem and cosmetic changes than substantive changes aimed at ending the climate of abuse."

Murphy saw some "resurrection" in this story of the women prisoners standing up for their rights as human beings. "Resurrection," she writes, "is practiced any time and in any place that oppressed people stand up and stand together to tell the unedited truth of their lives. ... The truth of the resurrection is this: that for however brief a time, women came together to tell the truth of their lives. One by one, they stood up and spoke it. . . . As they did this, they stood together, backing each other up because they knew it was the truth."

PROTEST AT THE NEW CITY JAIL, 1995

On October 2, 1981, city and business leaders in Atlanta stood in front of a "new" $14.2 million jail to dedicate it and celebrate how it would, in the words of then Mayor Maynard Jackson, "incorporate the most advanced concepts in public safety design anywhere in the nation." In 1991, shortly after the International Olympic Committee awarded the games to Atlanta, the City Council enacted three ordinances that outlawed (1) panhandling by "forcing oneself upon the company of another," (2) entering vacant buildings, and (3) walking across a parking lot without owning a vehicle that is parked there. The three ordinances were part of the "vagrant-free zone" efforts discussed in chapter nine. On January 31, 1995, city and business leaders in Atlanta stood in front of a "new" $67 million 1,000-bed jail officiously called the "Atlanta City Detention Center." Tom Pocock, director of Detention Center, declared the jail to be "the first Olympic project completed on time." Mayor Bill Campbell proclaimed how "humane" it would be.

Atlanta's jail expansion was part of a continuing national trend. By 2004, the U.S. had the largest documented prison population in the world, both in absolute and proportional terms with 2.03 million people behind bars, or 701 per 100,000 population. China had the second-largest number of prisoners (1.51 million, for a rate of 117 per 100,000), and Russia the second-highest rate (606 per 100,000, for a total of 865,000). If the number of persons on probation or parole are added, the number under the control of the criminal justice system goes up to nearly 7 million, or 3.2 percent of all U.S. adult residents, or 1 in every 32 adults.

Not surprisingly, the jails and prisons in the U.S., as is the case in Atlanta, were being filled by poor people and by people of color, and this has continued to the present. More than half of all prison and jail inmates have a reported annual income of less than $10,000 prior to their arrest. While roughly 80 percent of all U.S. men of working age are employed full-time, only 55 percent of state prison inmates were working full-time at the time of their arrest. It is estimated that 50 to 75 percent of all state prison inmates are unable to read. Only one-third of prisoners nationwide has completed high school. By contrast, of the general population, 85 percent of all men ages 20 to 29 have high school diplomas. In terms of race, according to the U.S. Department of Justice, by 2002, African American men were imprisoned at a rate of 4,810 per 100,000, Hispanic men at the rate of 1,740 per 100,000, and white men at a rate of 649 per 100,000.

When members of the Open Door Community and other protestors arrived for the "celebration" of the opening of Atlanta's new jail in 1995 they found the lectern with microphone and seating for the city and business elite already prepared but not yet occupied. Members of the community decided to begin the "celebration" early with some truth telling about how the jail would be "housing" the poor and people of color. Ed began the preaching, including some whooping and hollering and people began to respond with "Amens!" A revival meeting broke out, highlighting Jesus' teaching of identification with and liberation of the imprisoned. Riot police were called out to put down the preaching and testifying. An agreement was brokered to allow the city and business dignitaries their chance to speak, but also for the revival to continue at intervals. The city jail opened, but with an event that gave a different message than the one intended by the city.

Murphy points out that the "new" city jail, now over ten years old, was built to house the poor. One of its main functions is as a pre-trial detention center. This means those who are held there after arrest are those who cannot get bail or release on recognizance until there is a preliminary hearing. If at that hearing probable cause is found, the person is sent to one of the county jails. Only men and women convicted of a city ordinance violation will stay in the Atlanta City Detention Center. Every conviction of a city ordinance violation carries the choice between a fine and jail time (such as $120 or 30 days). Typically those who can afford to pay the fine do so and leave. Those who are left to do jail time are those who cannot afford to pay. Murphy comments:

> So in a strict sense, the post-conviction section of the Atlanta City Detention Center has been built exclusively for poor people. Those who do their time there will be those convicted of public urination, trespassing in a parking lot, disorderly conduct while intoxicated, street prostitution, aggressive panhandling, etc. Poor people's crimes. And poor people's time.

In the Open Door's analysis, the building of the new city jail immediately prior to the Olympics was no mere coincidence. As the Olympics approached, the police were called upon by the city government to do "sweeps" picking up homeless people, and charging them with "quality of life" ordinance violations, with the result that during the Olympics sizeable numbers of the homeless were behind bars. This is a pattern repeated for every major sports or convention event held in the city.

A study conducted by the Metro Atlanta Task Force for the Homeless supports the Open Door Community's analysis. The study concluded that the number of homeless arrests rises significantly just before large business conventions, most for violations of "status crimes." Another local organization, Cop-Watch, reported that during a convention of 35,000 Lutheran teenagers, eight police cars and two paddy wagons surrounded a centrally located park where many homeless people slept. Sergeant S. R. Traylor of the Atlanta Police Department explained to CopWatch that if the Christian students "see all of these homeless people, they'll never come back to Atlanta." Fridays are also a regular time for arresting the poor, because it ensures that they will remain in jail until their court date on Monday. Typically, the arresting officer does not show up for the hearing and the case is dropped. But the arrest had its intended effect: the defendant was removed from public sight for the weekend.

PHONE CAMPAIGN: COST OF COLLECT CALLS

Former resident volunteer Kristen Bargeron in a March 2000 *Hospitality* article, "Maximum Charges," detailed how the prison system works to cut off contact between those in prison and their family and friends and to increase state profits from those in prison. When a prisoner wants to make a phone call, it is a collect call. The prison system does not seek to get the lowest rates possible for this phone service. Rather, the system looks for the highest bidder, that is, the phone company that will charge the highest rates and give anywhere from 40–60 percent back to the state. Since there is one contract for an entire state prison system, the profits can be quite high for both the phone company and the state.

The prison system in Georgia, which has the 8th largest prison population in the nation (some 50,000 prisoners) provides an attractive phone market for phone companies. High rates mean high profits for the phone companies. Prison system defenders say that in Georgia the high rates help to fund programs for prisoners. But this is another example of how the system obscures the truth. What they do not point out is that public funds, tax dollars are used to fund these programs. The truth is thus less pleasant. Family members of prisoners, typically low income people, bear the cost of the "tax savings" for the general public.

The Open Door continues to publicize how the prison system exploits the family members of prisoners through high collect call rates.

CAMPAIGN FOR ABOLITION OF THE DEATH PENALTY

As we saw in chapter nine, the Open Door's history is replete with public actions that resist death by raising critical questions about the injustices the homeless suffer in Atlanta. We have already seen how these actions involve the community in controversy. Some who support the soup kitchen or other works of the community would prefer that soup be served without social critiques, that charity be given without attention to injustice. Still, those who make such criticisms usually share the Open Door's conviction that something is wrong in a society when people have no food or shelter and die on the streets from disease and exposure.

The Open Door's resistance to the death penalty, however, causes a sharper polarization. It commonly happened in the early years of the community that when an issue of *Hospitality* expressed the community's opposition to the death penalty, the next issue carried letters from persons stating that because of this opposition they would no longer support the community's work with the homeless. Often these letters ask why the community finds it even necessary to be involved with prison ministry and opposition to the death penalty. The community patiently explains that the work of hospitality with the homeless and the work of hospitality with those in prison, including work to end the death penalty, are all of one piece. All arise

VIGIL AT THE STATE CAPITOL, ATLANTA, 2005

from the loving and liberating life of Jesus Christ who stands with the hungry, the thirsty, the sick, the imprisoned, and who calls his disciples to "go and do likewise."

For each execution carried out by the state of Georgia, the Open Door Community stands with others in vigil at the state capital. The banners held are direct and simple: "Stop the Death Penalty," "Respect Life," and "End Executions." There is time for prayer, for songs of protest, for naming all of those the state has executed, and for quiet keeping of vigil. Strangely, this simple and subdued witness often enrages persons who drive by on their commute home, or on their way to a Braves baseball game. Seeing the faces of persons on their way to enjoy "America's Pastime" so contorted by anger at the presence of peaceful protestors makes one wonder what deep insecurities and anxieties are symbolized in the death penalty. The obscenities, gestures, and objects directed at the vigil participants seem to express a hatred and fear that can be satisfied only by the death of another human being. And the State, too, seems afraid to see these protesters question its business of death. At regular intervals Georgia State Patrol officers drive by the vigil. City police officers also sometimes take up positions across the street. Occasionally one notices men in conservative suits and wing-tip shoes observing the protest and taking pictures of the participants.

Participation by members of the Open Door Community and the raising of the incongruity between worshiping a crucified Lord and supporting the death penalty still raises the hackles of many within churches. At an execution vigil in January 2005, a local TV station interviewed Murphy Davis. A minister wrote Murphy stating:

> I saw you on tonight's newscast regarding the execution to be held today in Georgia. I must say as a Presbyterian I strongly disagree with your stance. I would suggest that rather than spending time trying to get in front of a camera that you should do actual ministry.

Ministers rarely preach against the death penalty, if they preach about it at all. Christian support for the death penalty remains high, and in the Bible Belt, even higher.

In the final analysis, the death penalty is the tip of the iceberg of prison life, both of which are degrading and dehumanizing. As politicians have whipped up a frenzy of fear of crime and scapegoating of prisoners, the number of executions has grown at the same time that longer and longer prison sentences with little or no effort at rehabilitation, and overcrowding have become the norm.

Through relationships with people who experience the unjust realities of the criminal justice system, the Open Door sees that both the streets and the prisons are populated by people relegated to the margins by a culture and social institutions organized around competition and self-interest. As we saw in chapter eight, the culture's "toilet assumption" deems certain persons disposable and flushes them away. On the streets and in prisons, the Open Door meets people whom society had consistently judged disposable and not worth the effort and the resources to help. Murphy explains:

> The death penalty is not an aberration of an otherwise good and just system. It is the finely honed expression of our deepest values. The death penalty is not only a grotesque reality in our system and cultural psyche, but it is a metaphor for our system, a sort of cultural icon in our psyche representing our soulless values. It is an icon that says, "People are objects: things to be disposed of at will, to be used up and thrown away."

To counter the "toilet assumption" and its dehumanizing results, Ed argues for a biblically based opposition to the death penalty. "The Bible" Ed insists, "is a book about the struggle and ultimate victory of life over death. Biblically informed people and traditions oppose death in all of its dehumanizing manifestations." He finds two biblical passages at the center of his belief and action: "I am now giving you the choice between life and death; between God's blessing and God's curse, and I call heaven and earth to witness the choice you make. Choose life" (Deuteronomy 30:19). And "Love never gives up" (1 Corinthians 13:7). Ed relates these "two biblical norms of commitment to life and the never-ending hope for forgiveness, reconciliation and new life" to the political necessities of "security of state (controlling violence against citizens)" and "the possibilities of major changes within the criminal justice system." He offers no easy answers, but calls for "a conversation" so that new possibilities can emerge to bring an end to the death penalty.

This conversation does not mean passivity. Ed writes that "as we wait for the concrete ways to work faithfully and lovingly in this world which belongs to our God, let us act." These actions are a mixture of personal conversion and public action:

First, we must pray for peace and the end of a system of violence and oppression. Also, we must live a life of resistance to the cultural values which choose death on so many levels of personal and national life. We need to write letters every week. First, get personally related to a death row prisoner by mail. Second, let us write to our representatives and newspaper editors especially concerning the cost and judicial chaos of the death penalty. Discover the role of your local district attorney. Does your D.A. work for life or death? At the terrible times of execution, please come to a vigil.

THE VAGRANT CHRIST,
MAUNDY THURSDAY, 2005

11

THE OPEN DOOR IN RELATION TO SOCIETY AND CHURCH

IN THE TWENTY-FIVE YEARS the Open Door Community has been at 910 Ponce de Leon, it is fair to say that the community's life, practice of hospitality, and political activism have provided an important alternative view to developments in the city of Atlanta, and in southern Christianity.

Looking back over this past quarter century, some would say that much has changed in the city of Atlanta. In the eyes of political and economic leaders, the city's downtown has undergone a remarkable transformation. Following the opening of Underground Atlanta in the late 1980s, there came in relatively quick succession the construction of a domed stadium, multiple sports facilities and housing for the 1996 Olympics, residential and commercial development, and an increased police presence. The business community has not fled the central city area. On the contrary, both business and residential construction has boomed as suburbanites began reversing a decades long trend of abandoning the city. The pride of the city over these developments seems far removed from the public doubt and anxiety expressed in the late 1970s and early 1980s. From the view of the political and business elite in Atlanta, the 1990s and early 2000s repeatedly confirmed Atlanta as one of the shining cities of the South, if not the entire nation.

The Open Door Community and other advocates for the homeless offer a contrary view of the past twenty-five years. For the political and economic powers, the Open Door offers troublesome reminders that this trumpeted prosperity has not improved the lives of the poor and homeless. And other signs that continue to cloud attempts to present a picture of prosperity for all confirm the view of the Open Door. According to the Metro Atlanta Task for the Homeless, Atlanta lost 9,000 units of "affordable" housing during 1995–96. The Housing Wage in Georgia is $14.00. This is the amount a full time (40 hours per week) worker must earn per hour in order to afford a two-bedroom unit at the area's Fair Market rent. In Atlanta, 18,000 to 19,000 people are typically cited for "quality of life" violations in one year. Atlanta was cited as being the "3rd meanest" city in the country in the 2002 Criminalization Report, published by the National Coalition for the Homeless. In the two months of December 2004 and January 2005, three homeless men known by the Open Door died from illnesses related to being on the streets. At each Monday and Tuesday breakfast, the Open Door regularly serves 120 or more homeless people, and about the same number at each soup kitchen on Wednesday and Thursday. Homeless people are still routinely arrested for public urination, while the city of Atlanta still refuses to provide any public toilets. The city jail is full of poor people, and in state prisons and on death row, most of those locked up are poor and disproportionately black.

The contrast in perceptions between those holding political and economic power and those on the underside is not unique to Atlanta. This difference is, in fact, paradigmatic of developments in the United States which mark the last decade and contain ominous implications for the future. In simplest terms, the rich have been getting richer and the poor have been getting poorer. The middle class, meanwhile, has experienced an increasing financial squeeze. The House Ways and Means Committee reported in the fall of 1990 that between 1979 and 1987 the poorest fifth of American families became 9 percent poorer and the richest fifth became 19 percent richer. A report by the Center on Budget and Policy Priorities showed that the richest 1 percent saw their income grow 87 percent while the take home pay of the poorest fifth fell 5.2 percent. By the end of the decade, the poorest fifth of the American people was left with less than 5 percent of the nation's income while the richest fifth grabbed more than 40 percent. These trends continued as the new millennium unfolded. The Economic Policy Institute drawing upon Census data reports that the numbers of people in poverty have risen since 2000 with 5.4 million more persons, including 1.4 million children added to the poverty rolls. This Institute also notes the continuing unbalanced nature of the U.S. economy with "the share of total national income flowing to the bottom 60 percent of households was essentially unchanged," while "the share going to the top 5 percent was up 0.4 percentage points, from 21.4 percent to 21.8 percent. As of 2004, the top fifth of households held 50.1 percent of all income, tied with 2001 for the highest share on record."

The Open Door confronts daily what the economic and political powerful want to hide and deny: the economic policies of the ruling elite in this country are crushing the poor. The Open Door argues that both the growing number of people out on the streets and the bulging prison population across the nation reflects an economic system failing to serve human needs. Increasing numbers of people are being excluded from meaningful participation in both the economic and political life of the nation.

Those who started the Open Door, and those who have joined the community over the years, are part of a public Christian response to this injustice and oppression in our society. The Open Door Community is but one of many intentional Christian communities across the United States. Together they resist and condemn an economic system and governmental policies based on the assumption that prosperity for all results from favoring a few.

More mainline Christian voices have also been highly critical of the direction of economic and political life in the United States. The Roman Catholic Bishops of the United States, for example, stated in their 1986 pastoral letter on the U.S. economy that "the precarious economic situation of so many people and so many families calls for examination of U.S. economic arrangements." "That so many people are poor in a nation as rich as ours," the bishops continued, "is a social and moral scandal that we cannot ignore."

The Open Door Community in its life and work believe, however, that it is not enough to issue policy statements; what is needed are communities that embody the principles and virtues of those statements. Community members consistently state in their deeds and their words that when people must stand in line for food, for shelter, or for a shower and clothes, there is something fundamentally wrong in our economic system. In the same light, the community finds that there is something terribly askew when the only solution to violence our political system can uncover is further violence in the form of dehumanizing prison conditions and executions. People of faith cannot stand idle in the face of these conditions and abdicate their responsibility to the state.

But what alternative does the Open Door offer for the future? The Open Door sees that its primary task is to live the Gospel faithfully, and only out of that commitment can it act and speak. As a small community, its own actions remain focused on the local level even as it sees its battle as part of a struggle against systems of oppression. The community believes that its engagement in specific actions aimed at accomplishing specific goals on behalf of the homeless or imprisoned are necessary steps toward larger systemic change. The daily practice of the works of mercy seeks to build relationships with the poor and to meet their most immediate needs. Actions such as the takeover of the Imperial Hotel are immediately directed toward the creation of single occupancy residential housing. The Grady Campaign illustrates not only the health care crisis in Atlanta, but also the need for a serious overhaul of the business of medicine in the United States in order to assure basic health care for all.

At other times, we have seen the Open Door seek in its actions such achievable goals as public restrooms in the downtown area, replacements for park space lost to construction, and the opening of shelters by the city. All of these actions bring some change at the local level while also reminding people that a broad social response to the needs of the poor and the homeless must be put on the state and national agenda. Through demonstrations and speaking at churches, public meetings, schools, or in the streets, community members continually seek to make people aware of the connections between poverty, race, and the use of the death penalty in the United States.

If anything is clear from the history of the Open Door, it is that these efforts for justice are central to the life of the community. We have seen that their wholistic spirituality and ethic insists that mercy and justice cannot be separated without both becoming distorted. Love both presupposes and surpasses justice. Thus justice is really an expression of love in structural and institutional form. The love of the Open Door Community for people on the streets or in prisons is grounded in the love of Christ. Christ's love expressed in his life and death shattered social boundaries intended to exclude persons from fully sharing in life. In the actions and words of Christ, all persons are invited to share in the fullness of God's creation. At the banquet in the Beloved Community, all are welcomed and fed. This vision sustains the actions of the community on behalf of justice. Because they have received life from the gracious acts of God, they seek to give freely, to seek the good of others in justice. For the same reasons, the more personal actions of visiting a prisoner or serving soup to a homeless person are grounded in Christ's love. Christ comes in the guise of the stranger.

As the Open Door looks upon its twenty-five year history and considers what may lie ahead, it fully recognizes the difficulty of sustaining the vision of Christ in the stranger who is homeless or on death row. It is, the community confesses, impossible without God. Members of the Open Door can see Christ in the homeless person or the prisoner on death row because God gives them this vision. This vision has deep biblical roots. In the Hebrew scriptures, the Israelites are told: "You shall not oppress a stranger; you know the heart of a stranger for you were strangers in the land of Egypt" (Exodus 23:9). Throughout the Hebrew scriptures, faithfulness to God's covenant is judged by treatment of strangers (Deuteronomy 10:18–19, Psalm 146:9, Jeremiah 7:6, Ezekiel 22:29). In Matthew 25, Jesus tells the crowd and his disciples: "When you did this to the least of these, you did it to me." On the road to Emmaus, the resurrected Christ appears to two disciples.

They do not recognize him until the breaking of the bread. The author of the letter to the Hebrews writes: "Let love for one another continue. Do not neglect to show hospitality to strangers, for thereby some have entertained angels unawares" (Hebrews 13:1–2). Paul writes the Corinthians: "God gives to the poor. God's justice endures forever. God who supplies seed to the sower and bread for food will supply and multiply your seed and cause the harvest of your justice to continue" (2 Corinthians 9:9–10).

In this spirit of the scriptures, community members find that their prayer is made fervent by their work. When they share the bread of the Eucharist, they share the food of the soup kitchen. When they wash each other's feet, they are cleansed with those in the shower line. When they join hands to share their hopes and fears, their concerns come from the streets and prisons. Murphy stresses that the community's work, in which they seek to see Christ under the guise of the stranger, requires that it be a worshiping community:

> If we were not persons of faith we wouldn't have the resources to deal with an execution of a friend. We wouldn't have the resources to face the line at our door every day. Prayer, sacrament, worship—are central. We have to work out of a context in which the belief that healing is possible is central. Our grief is shared, just as our joy is. God's heart is breaking too when we execute a person, when we turn a person away because the soup kitchen has ended. That breaks God's heart. And that's the God we serve—a God with a broken heart.

The Open Door believes that Christians can and ought to be concerned about social policies, about institutional change, and large scale efforts to create a more just society. But this focus on broad social change in the future should not become an excuse for personal inaction now. The big changes come slowly. Meanwhile persons are suffering and dying in our streets and prisons. Rather than despair because the structures of economic and political life seem deaf to the cries of those on the margins, the community calls for patient work and public activism sustained by relationships with homeless and imprisoned persons. The Open Door believes that to give in to the powers of death, to say all action in service or protest is fruitless, denies faith in the life-giving liberation of Jesus Christ.

In this spirit of resistance Elizabeth Dede suggests three steps ordinary persons can take to begin making changes to end homelessness and abolish the death penalty. The first is to stop measuring our lives in terms of material success. She writes:

> We simply are not following Jesus' teachings when we are concerned with things. Luke records that Jesus taught his followers "Happy are you poor; the kingdom of God is yours." . . . If we are Christians we are supposed to be seeking God's kingdom. Yet most of us are not poor or hungry, and many of us do not have active involvement with the poor and hungry. If our lives are filled with material goods we should be concerned, I think, because God is going to send us away empty. In fact, we probably already are empty because our shallow lives have missed the depths of God's love for the hungry and the poor.

In the second step, she stresses that "we must begin to act in ways that recognize Jesus' presence in our lives now." Her logic is simple: "Jesus identifies himself with the least, so if we are to see Jesus, we must look among the poor and needy, and if we want to be with Jesus, then we must be with the poor."

Finally it is necessary to build a community that will provide a base of support in the daily taking of these steps.

Elizabeth recalls the example of the early church described in the second chapter of Acts:

> All the believers continued together in close fellowship and shared their belongings with one another. They would sell their property and possessions, and distribute the money among all, according to what each one needed. Day after day they met as a group in the Temple, and they had their meals together in their homes, eating with glad and humble hearts, praising God, and enjoying the good will of all the people (Acts 2:44–47).

She finds that this biblical account seriously questions whether Christian communities can rest easy with a capitalism that "bleeds the life out of some while others prosper at a disproportionate rate." Elizabeth concludes by asking us to imagine "the joyous feasts that would take place in Atlanta if the lonely developers of Underground would share their evening dinners with the hungry and homeless of Atlanta."

The faith-formed community life and resistance of the Open Door not only stands in tension with American society, it also reflects, reinterprets, and in some ways resists major characteristics of the dominant form of religion in the South. Charles Reagan Wilson identifies southern Christianity as dominated by Protestantism. This dominance is clearly evident in the Open Door's history in terms of support, forms of worship, and ongoing inspiration for the life of the community.

From its beginning with four white Presbyterians at Clifton Presbyterian Church, two of whom were Presbyterian ministers, the Open Door has been anchored in Protestantism. Most of the residents, resident volunteers, and partners over the years have been Protestants. The Atlanta Presbytery, and many individual Presbyterian and other Protestant churches have from the beginning supported the community, both financially and with people who volunteer with the community.

The community's worship also reflects a continuing reliance upon southern Protestantism. Daily prayer and Sunday worship are centered around the Bible and personal experiences and needs, with very little set formal prayer. Most of the music in worship is drawn from spirituals and folk or protest music.

The community's origins and ongoing life also draw inspiration from the example and history of alternative Protestant communities in the South such as Clarence Jordan's Koinonia Farm in Americus, Georgia. Further southern Protestant inspiration comes from persons and organizations such as Will Campbell and the Committee of Southern Churchmen, Martin Luther King, Jr., and the Southern Christian Leadership Conference (SCLC), and Concerned Black Clergy, an organization of progressive Black ministers in Atlanta.

At the same time, however, the Open Door reflects in its support, prayer, and inspiration an opening to Catholicism and other denominations that indicates a loosening of Protestant hegemony in the South. The community receives financial and volunteer support from Catholic Church members, and many non-Christians. Members of the community have included Catholics, Mennonites, those without a specific denominational affiliation, and occasionally non-Christians, such as Muslims, Buddhists, and Jews.

In terms of prayer, we have seen that the Open Door differs from the typical Protestant practice of monthly or even less occasional celebrations of the Eucharist, in that the community has this service each Sunday. Yet the Lord's Supper at the Open Door remains distinctively Protestant in having time for sharing of concerns and personal prayer, spirituals, an emphasis upon preaching the Word, and a rotating leadership of the service itself.

In terms of inspiration, Dorothy Day and the Catholic Worker movement deeply influenced the founders of the community, and this influence has continued to grow over the years. The community has come to call itself a "Protestant Catholic Worker House," and has increased participation in Catholic Worker events and collaboration with Catholic Worker communities. Its life is structured much like a Catholic Worker house, including time each week for what Dorothy Day called "clarification of thought" and the linking of direct service to the poor with protest actions urging justice for homeless people and against the death penalty and war.

The second major characteristic Wilson identifies in southern Christianity is an experiential faith focused on sin, Christ's atoning death, and salvation experienced as conversion.

We have seen that the Open Door emerged out of an experientially focused faith life among members of Clifton Presbyterian Church. A Bible study at the church led the four eventual founders of the Open Door to be with and to serve the poor, to enter into a prison ministry and offering meals and shelter to homeless people. The desire to include solidarity with the poor with this integration of spirituality and service led the founders to take the next step and begin the Open Door.

Faith life within the Open Door reflects a traditional southern Christianity emphasis upon intense experiential faith, sin, the cross, and conversion, but these are radically transformed by an emphasis upon solidarity with the poor and social action. We have seen a consistent willingness of the community to identify and confess its own shortcomings and sins, and to repent by making changes in the life of the community. Community members acknowledge the same in their own personal lives within the community. As Ed indicates "The difference [between the Open Door and society] is not in the presence or absence of sin and iniquity, but in our response to its presence and power in our lives." That response is a continual effort at conversion from this sin.

In this conversion, the Open Door sees the cross at the heart of a Christian faith as it urges that homelessness is the crucifixion of the poor and the death penalty is the continuation of crucifixion. The community links the meaning of Jesus' death on the cross with the sinfulness of persons and social structures that make for the suffering of homeless people and the execution of prisoners. In the cries of the poor and the prisoner, the community believes the prophetic call to conversion is given. Conversion means turning from selfishness, greed, and self-righteousness to "the ever-flowing mercy of a loving God," and turning toward solidarity with the poor, serving homeless people and prisoners, and struggling against a system that supports homelessness and executions.

The third major characteristic of southern Christianity is a fundamentalist literalism in regard to the Bible that is, however, focused on individual salvation.

The Open Door takes the Bible seriously. The community emerged out of biblical study linked with engagement with the poor and the Bible has remained central to the Open Door. In particular, we have seen that Matthew 25 and Isaiah 58, are repeatedly emphasized as God's Word calling members to be with and serve the poor. Both of these texts emphasize the importance of serving God through serving the "least of these" and in particular to feed the hungry, shelter the homeless, visit the prisoner, and seek justice for the poor. These texts serve as a charter for the Open Door's life and work.

Biblical passages are read and discussed before serving the homeless at breakfast, or in the soup kitchen. Biblical stories are directly related to the life and the work of the community. Jesus' feeding the multitudes is related to the breakfast. Jesus eating with outcasts is equated with the soup kitchen. Jesus' healings are linked with the free medical clinic at the Open

Door and with protests against budget cuts for Grady Hospital. Prophetic judgments upon injustice are expressed in demonstrations and in articles in the community's newspaper, *Hospitality*. Community members turn to the Bible to analyze the life of the community, and political, economic, and cultural life in the United States.

At the same time, the Open Door sees itself as critical of both fundamentalism and a kind of "liberal" biblical theology. Ed Loring states, for example, that "for the majority of Southern Baptists, the 'completely inspired word of God without fault or error' basically means that they are safe members of the Republican Party. The white middle-class American way of life is the real standard-bearer." He points to a contradiction in fundamentalism, "Every word is fully inspired and is as authoritative for science as for doctrine! Yet the[y] do not take a stand against charging interest on loans to the poor—a precept that fills the pages of the Old Testament. Also, [they] support the death penalty for homicide . . . but they do not stone to death rebellious sons and adultery-committing wives." The Open Door sees fundamentalism's focus on individual salvation and its absence of solidarity with the poor and struggle for justice and liberation as inconsistent with Jesus' life and teaching.

In regard to the "liberal biblical theology," Loring writes, "The only way to 'know' the Bible and to test the authenticity of its contents is to live it. The streets, not the university, are the place to discover the word of God." Liberals are too willing to throw money at problems from a distance while they resist essential change in social institutions. He sees both liberal biblical theology and the fundamentalists as ending up "at about the same place, as defenders of the status quo in a sea of injustice."

The fourth major characteristic Wilson identifies in southern Christianity is an individualistic moralism in which Christian holiness is equated with purity defined by avoiding sins having primarily to do with individual vices such as drinking, dancing, gambling, and more recently homosexuality and abortion.

Within the Open Door there is an emphasis upon refraining from personal vices that on the surface appears quite consistent with this moralism. Members are told that tight-fitting or revealing clothes and short skirts are inappropriate, and that the Open Door does not condone sex/sleeping together outside of a covenant relationship. Further, drinking of alcoholic beverages is not allowed within the residence. Smoking is discouraged and those who do smoke are required to do so outside. Watching television is banned within the house.

Yet these practices are not about individual purity. Rather, the community connects restraint from personal vice with solidarity with the poor, disciplines necessary for both personal and social liberation. Inappropriate sexual relations harm the community's own harmony and thus its ability to serve the poor. Given the addictions to alcohol and/or drugs of many community members, the ban on alcohol is seen as supporting liberation from addiction. The same emphasis is present in the discouragement of smoking. Television is viewed as a means of enticing conformity to the dominant social values of consumerism and violence. The community tells incoming residents, "We strive to live simply and recognize that two-thirds of the world eat meals without meat, have little to wear, do not shop at malls, and they use public transportation, or walk. . . . The World of Coke and Underground Atlanta are not appropriate tour sites, because of our political/cultural resistance to the American Empire. However, the City Jail, Woodruff Park, the King Center, the High Museum, and Grady Hospital are important places to visit."

Wilson's fifth characteristic of southern Christianity is a focus on an interior religiousity expressed in emotional displays of faith rather than social change. Samuel Hill brings some nuance to this statement in recognizing that this religiousity reflects a southern emphasis upon conversion, and so efforts at social change are tied into conversion.

Further, Hill identifies four types of religious activism in Southern Christianity, all of which aim at social change through conversion, but have different strategies for urging conversion. Of the four, two of these types intersect with the Open Door's approach to social change: direct; and oblique.

These two types share a more intentional political stance as a means to conversion and social change. The direct type aims at specific political and economic change, but they seek conversion as the basis for this change. The direct type has taken various organizational forms, such as the Southern Tenant Farmer's Union and the Southern Christian Leadership Conference (SCLC). The "conversionist" bent of the direct type is evident, for example, when we recall that the slogan of the SCLC was, "To Redeem the Soul of America."

The oblique type consists of radical Christians who embody in their lives a prophetic critique. They seek to live an alternative to the dominant norms of southern Christian life as a means of a calling themselves and others to conversion. Will Campbell, a white Southern Baptist civil rights activist and Clarence Jordan, the founder of Koinonia Farm, who are both important inspirational figures for the Open Door, are examples of this type.

The Open Door in its emphasis upon community life organized as an alternative to larger society is easily identified with the oblique type. The Open Door integrates efforts for justice with direct personal involvement with the poor and imprisoned. The serving of the poor through food, clothing, showers, and serving the needs of prisoners is ongoing. The community seeks in its life to embody the change it urges for the entire society. Further, the community believes its passion for justice is stirred through personal relationship with those who are poor and imprisoned.

At the same time, the Open Door also has elements of the direct type as it seeks specific economic and political change while retaining an emphasis upon conversion. Ed reflects the emphasis upon conversion when he observes that "Through speaking engagements, legislative lobbying, Bible study, and public protests, the Open Door attempts to change human hearts and human law toward life-sustaining structures of justice." We have seen in its many creative and highly publicized protests over the years how the Open Door reflects the direct type. From carrying toilets into the Mayor's office to protest for public toilets, to the takeover of the Imperial Hotel, to the Grady Campaign, to vigils against executions, the community consistently gives public witness to its vision of the Beloved Community.

We have also seen how this direct advocacy takes the form of prayer services so that the powerful emotional content of worship is integrated with efforts for social change. The Open Door's liturgical calendar includes worship done at sites around the city, at least twice a year, during Holy Week and again in September during the "Festival of Shelters."

Wilson's sixth characteristic of southern Christianity is that it tends to support or at least not challenge racial and economic injustice. Though recognizing that this characteristic has to be qualified in light of Hill's analysis of approaches to social change within southern Christianity, it generally holds. Most of white southern Christianity has not been identified with progressive social transformation.

The Open Door sees itself in a struggle against this aspect of southern Christianity. Murphy criticizes a southern Protestant Christianity in which, "you can go to church and confess to all the creeds . . . and at the same time you can make bombs, plan wars, hate Willie Horton, oppress your workers." In this Christianity, she says, "I'm afraid that while we're deeply pained by a breach of manners, we're not pained enough by oppression and the death-dealing power of oppression in the lives of the poor." In contrast, Murphy states, the Open Door sees that "When we receive the grace of . . . freedom, our life and our doctrine become one . . . we walk the way of the Prince of Peace, who walks with us and shepherds us to bring good news to the poor, liberty to the captives, recovery of sight to the blind; to set free the oppressed; and to announce that the time has come when God will save her people."

Ed sees the failure of southern Christianity to confront social injustice as traceable, among other sources, to its individualistic emphasis upon justification by faith alone. He states, "Justification by faith alone . . . has undergirded slavery, racism, capitalism, sexism, war . . . Justification by grace is clearly biblical. Alone it is an ideological tool for the defense of power and abuse." Ed urges a discipleship that lives out the social implications of justification. He states, "Since 'none are righteous, no not one,' no person can say 'I am better.' No one can say, 'I deserve more because I am more talented or I have worked harder.' No one can say, 'I am more important because I own more, or I am more educated. . . .' Given this radical equality in the eyes of God, we Christians . . . do not all seek to be the same, rather we work to prevent the using of our differences to justify structures of dominance."

The community itself has intentionally sought to have racial and class diversity and to structure its life together to address class, race, and gender differences within the community. We have seen how the community has struggled to make its own lines of authority and decision-making inclusive and not repeat the class and race divisions of the larger society. However, there are still tensions and conflicts within the community that reflect racial and class differences.

This analysis of the Open Door's history in relation to six major characteristics of Southern Christianity reveals that the Open Door draws upon, reflects, and transforms those characteristics. Its origins, support, and inspiration reflect continuity with southern Christianity and an opening to other forms of Christianity. Its theology takes typical emphases upon experiential faith, sin, atonement, and the Bible, and reworks them to support solidarity with and service to the poor, especially homeless persons and those in prison. Its political activism reflects a traditional emphasis upon conversion, and minority Southern traditions that urge conversion through direct action and communal witness. The vitality of the community over its twenty five years of history and its influence within the religious and political life of Atlanta likely has much to do with its ability to draw upon, rework, and criticize various elements of Southern Christianity.

Given its struggles with both society and church in America, community members admit that it is unlikely that its vision of a joyous feast in which everybody has enough, in which "all God's children have shoes," representing the Beloved Community, will occur in the near future. But the community believes that when they serve breakfast or soup at 910, or offer showers and a change of clothes, signs of the Beloved Community are present. If the structures of injustice in both society and church are resistant to change, the community seeks in love to keep pushing and hoping for transformation. This kind of love serves and presses for justice.

In this history, we have traced the daily steps the Open Door Community takes toward liberation, toward the transformation of the powers of sin and death into powers of reconciliation and new life, two steps of which would be the abolition of homelessness and the death penalty. Along the way we have seen the Open Door witness to the conversion and liberation they seek for themselves and for our whole society. It is a conversion which promotes awareness of injustice while concretely engaging in works of reconciliation. By their life together, the Open Door Community challenges the numerous forms of enslavement our society promotes: consumerism, the security of weapons, racism, sexism, and prisons. They ask us to come to our senses, to repent.

Repentance is the first step toward reconciliation and the creation of community. The Open Door invites this repentance through the recognition of our common redemption in Jesus Christ. Jesus' suffering and death witnesses to the fact that reconciliation does not come easily because the hurt and injustice are profound. Reconciliation demands change that is often costly. There cannot be reconciliation without repentance. Thus the Open Door Community struggles to provide a place for repentance and reconciliation, a home where forgiveness can be shared. The community welcomes Christ who comes in the guise of the stranger and invites others to do the same.

As a community that grows out of Jesus' call to conversion, the Open Door describes itself as on a pilgrimage toward the Beloved Community. There is a sense of wandering in the desert after beginning with the great moment of liberation. The New Testament tension, the reality of the Reign of God present and the not yet of the Reign of God to come, is strongly felt in the Open Door Community. The very name of the community testifies to this eschatological tension. At the Open Door, the doors remain closed and locked when community members need to rest at night. Still they work and hope for the day when all locks and keys will disappear. In this community, African American, Hispanic and white, rich and poor, educated and uneducated, gay and straight, women and men attempt to dismantle the barriers of inequality and oppression and build the beloved community. The barriers are strong. They have not all been overcome in the Open Door. The conversion still takes place, the new reality in Christ is acknowledged, even as the struggle continues with the principalities and powers.

This is the work the Open Door Community embraces as a result of conversion: to affirm the humanity of the homeless, of the imprisoned, and of those on death row by recognizing them as fellow children of God. This recognition means sharing life together in the love of Christ and the mutuality of human dignity he brings. The community stands with two of the open sores in American society: those places where the homeless and imprisoned are marginalized and condemned. Even though homelessness has received some public attention, few people seem willing to begin the serious work necessary to get at the causes and structures creating and sustaining it. The moral imagination, the vision of life necessary to achieve such changes is still lacking among political leaders, and most Christians. The homeless are still seen as non-persons, as threats to the downtown shoppers and business, and as a problem for bureaucrats to solve.

The death penalty receives public attention in the form of sensationalism in media reporting around executions. Vengeance has become ever more popular as our way of life appears threatened on so many sides. In this context, it has perhaps become increasingly scandalous to ask, as the Open Door does, whether vengeance heals any wounds, or brings any reconciliation. Again, the moral imagination is lacking to see the death penalty as a tool to control the poor and African-Americans and as a basic affront to human dignity. In prayer, protest, and by coming to know those on death row as persons, the community seeks to stir the conscience of society and to hold to the hope of forgiveness and reconciliation.

Since the Open Door Community is led into its work by conversion and life with the poor, it is also sustained in that work by prayer and worship. The Eucharist flows out of the soup kitchen, the shower lines, and the prisons where Christ is met under the guise of the stranger. Without prayer, the work would grow burdensome, the disappointments would lead to discouragement, the Gospel vision of God's reign would be dimmed. The activism of the community is rooted in the

ADVENT, 2004

power of prayer, of meeting God in silence, in sacrament, in the Word, and in the poor. Their life in common has integrity as their work and worship are bound together in service to God. This remains the gracious source of the Open Door's life and its continuous striving to live faithfully to the vision of the Beloved Community in which the bread of life is shared as all are welcomed at God's banquet table.

Also available from the Open Door

A WORK OF HOSPITALITY. THE OPEN DOOR READER, 1982–2002. Peter R. Gathje, editor. The twentieth-anniversary collection of essays, sermons, meditations, and poetry from the community's newspaper, *Hospitality*. 370 pp., including Open Door time line and reading list. ISBN 0-9715893-0-5. Suggested donation: **$15.00.**

I HEAR HOPE BANGING AT MY BACK DOOR. WRITINGS FROM HOSPITALITY. By Ed Loring, with a foreword by Rev. Timothy McDonald III. A collection of 12 essays. 77 pp. Suggested donation: **$10.00.**

TO ORDER

Orders may be requested by phone, fax, or in writing. Or, visit our website, www.opendoorcommunity.org.

The Open Door Community
910 Ponce de Leon Avenue, N.E.
Atlanta, GA 30306
Phone: (404) 874-9652
Fax: (404) 874-7964

Shipping and handling is included in the suggested prices above. As always, there is special pricing for bulk orders. If funds are not available, books will be sent at no cost.

Subscribing to *Hospitality,* our monthly newspaper, is free.

Martin Luther King Campaign for Economic Justice

THE MARTIN LUTHER KING CAMPAIGN is the justice and resistance organizing arm of the Open Door Community. We seek members who are interested in shouting, marching, singing, preaching, picketing and putting your bodies in the way of the powers that are crushing the poor of our city. Please come and join us in our works of justice. The Martin Luther King Campaign for Economic Justice was established April 4, 2005, the anniversary of Dr. King's martyrdom, as a movement for economic justice and no war in the city of King's birth Atlanta, Georgia. From King's blood and life we will flow into the streets of Atlanta to disrupt business as usual until the hungry have food, until the homeless are housed, until the County Prosecutor is opposed to the death penalty, until the churches make a preferential option for the poor, until all laws harming the homeless are off the books, until public toilets are accessible for all God's children, until every gay and lesbian person is accorded equal rights in the political domain and churches, until Grady hospital is funded at 100% of county assessment in DeKalb and Fulton counties, and until all our public officials, rabbis and imams are happy and hopeful human beings who act out of compassion and love for the poor. The establishment of the Beloved Community which was King's revolutionary vision during the last three years of his life, is our aim and purpose. Come, join us, the Beloved Community awaits!

Southern Prison Ministry

SOUTHERN PRISON MINISTRY was founded by Murphy Davis in 1977 in partnership with the Committee of Southern Churchfolk, an interracial ecumenical ministry founded in the 1960s by Will Campbell. When the Open Door was founded in 1981, Southern Prison Ministry became a part of the community's work. We have from the beginning, emphasized in our work visitation with women in the state prison system and the men, women and children on death row in Georgia. We advocate and agitate for the abolition of the death penalty and mass imprisonment.

As prisons in the United States swell up and swallow thousands more people than in any other time or place in human history, we respond to the call to "Remember the prisoners as if you were in prison with them" (Hebrews 13). There are now more than 80,000 prisoners (not counting the children) in the state of Georgia—a five-fold increase since our work began. We name and engage the idol of institutional punishment in the mad rush to build and fill prisons in response to every community problem. We decry warehousing the mentally ill in prison and the vast increase in private profits from the punishment industry. And we challenge the church to think critically and theologically about this disastrous path and to respond as the frenzy of incarceration blows up in our faces. Through the monthly trips to transport families and friends to visit the prisons at Hardwick and Jackson, GA, through prisoner advocacy, research, writing, and public actions against the death penalty, we provide ways for hundreds of concerned folk to engage and resist.